The Guns Nobody Heard

23 Years That Changed America Forever

Joe James

PublishAmerica
Baltimore

© 2007 by Joe James.
All rights reserved. No part of this book may be reproduced, stored in a retrieval system or transmitted in any form or by any means without the prior written permission of the publishers, except by a reviewer who may quote brief passages in a review to be printed in a newspaper, magazine or journal.

First printing

ISBN: 1-4241-5404-9
PUBLISHED BY PUBLISHAMERICA, LLLP
www.publishamerica.com
Baltimore

Printed in the United States of America

This is not fiction but about real people in an often turbulent and unique time. Names have been changed in situations like pursuit of the suspected German spy in Barbados. By some chance he may have escaped the British and now heads up a thriving business in Hamburg.

Acknowledgments

Thanks to Dean Neugent, for bakery facts; PR pro Richard Brown, who was there; Michael James for editing; Gerry Law Jr. and Ian Ruder for computer know how; Mark James for help along the way, Olive and Gerry Law for photos, and Calvin Clyde for telling me about PublishAmerica. And to Peggy James for patience and encouragement over 63 ongoing years.

Foreword

Uncle Ed used to say, "Things can be going pretty good until some idiot leaves the gate open." We were struggling to get out of the Depression when Hitler kicked open some gates and left all of them open. We didn't pay much attention since it wasn't our cattle. Then another gate got smashed open out in Hawaii and we were in it.

When the war was over, we picked up where we left off. You don't go fight for five years and come home to find everything smooth as a baby's butt. If you wanted to buy a car there was a three month wait. The fact that you were a returning hero wasn't worth squat.

All kinds of new gadgets were coming out like televisions, refrigerators, and air conditioning. Not that most of us returning Texas vets could afford them. But we pitched in and scrambled to find jobs. And slowly things got better. A sort of tranquility settled over Texas and the nation.

For almost twenty-five years, nobody "left the gate open" and we had time to "get on with it." It was sort of a "time between," a blissful innocence with no apprehension about the future. We had time to find jobs or start a business and even to have fun with our young families.

Then a mail order rifle flashed on Elm Street and our unique and peaceful era ended.

Texas and the rest of America would never again know the tranquility we enjoyed for 23 years.

The Guns Nobody Heard

Sometimes, not always, professors speak words of infinite wisdom. In his University of Texas classroom, geology professor Arthur Dean lamented the ongoing construction of the Golden Gate bridge. "They are building it right on the fault line," he protested. That was 1939. At last check the bridge was still there.

That same year twinkle-eyed Professor Robert P. Crawford, visiting from the University of Nebraska, ignored any concern about the Golden Gate Bridge. Usually with a bubbly and happy outlook about people and journalism, Crawford's mood changed when Hitler invaded Poland. "This," he announced solemnly, "is the start of a hundred years of warfare."

His about-to-graduate students chuckled at such a preposterous prediction. The war in Europe was of little concern. Hitler was a pompous little man with a weird cowlick. His war was three thousand miles away across a surging

Atlantic no army could cross. There were more serious concerns, like finding a job. The Depression was still with us, smothering Texas and the rest of America in a fog of grinding frustration. Engineering grads, deftly swinging slide rules, could not find an engineer job. The only engineers working, the joke went, were driving railroad engines and got laid off frequently. Architects found no buildings to design and if a journalism grad found a job it paid fifteen dollars a week.

"You should have been here yesterday," Professor Thompson said rather sadly. "Fellow was in here from Keystone View. That's an outfit up in Pennsylvania. He needs an assistant to go with an author. Traveling in South America. You speak Spanish. You would have been a natural for the job."

A job! An honest to goodness job? And now the man was gone.

The professor nodded sadly. Yes, the man was on his way back to Pennsylvania. Then the professor brightened. "I guess if you want the job you could go up there."

He didn't suggest using a telephone. Just go up there and see that man before he hired somebody else.

No thought of train or bus. That would cost money few graduates had. Pack that battered suitcase, get out on the highway, and start waving a thumb.

Today few people hitchhike. And for good reason. Not many people will pick up a hitchhiker.

In 1940, with so many people unemployed, people with cars picked up hitchhikers. "You look like an honest person to me," a car owner would say as you climbed in. What he really meant was "I sure hope you are not going to rob me. I'm taking a chance." Highway speeds were 45 to 50 miles an hour, so drivers had time to look over a hitchhiker. Often a car would pass, then back up. So maybe they sized us up and got a final look as they passed.

THE GUNS NOBODY HEARD
23 YEARS THAT CHANGED AMERICA FOREVER

Almost every driver who picked up a hitch hiker was a non stop talker. Here was a chance to brag to a captive audience. Usually the driver was alone and talked incessantly—about himself.

Listening was the price one paid for the ride.

Heading north, a hitch hiker walked or got a ride to the north side of each town. Who got there early claimed the first position. The next arrival nodded in acknowledgment and walked farther north to a good spot. Often four or five hitchhikers flanked the highway out of town. One hoped to be the neatest looking and attract the driver who passed the others. If that failed you waited until the first hiker got a ride. Then move up one spot. As the sun lowered this became a nervous wait.

Rain pattered and darkness neared when a driver dropped me in Greenville, South Carolina. "There's a little motel over there," he said kindly, assuming I had the price. I had the buck fifty, paid the man behind the battered counter, and flopped wearily into bed. A knock on the door and I sat bolt upright.

The door opened and a lady, bosomy in the hall light, said, "Hello baby! Can I come in?"

"No!" I protested. "Please go away. I'm dead tired."

She shrugged and left. But constant laughter and giggles up and down that hallway lasted all night long. The motel was not exactly a motel.

One driver solved the hotel problem. He was a dashing sort of fellow who sold phonograph records. As we approached Washington, D.C. he told of a new talent sure to sell a lot of records. "Name's Crosby," he promised. "They call him Bing. Really got a voice." Maybe but back home nobody heard of Bing. Jimmy Davis, Bob Wills or Ernest Tubb for sure, but nobody with a name like Bing.

It was misty rain when the music man stopped at a plush downtown hotel. "You can bunk with me if you want to," he said. "Won't cost you nothing."

A warning flag went up. I heard about strangers a hitchhiker didn't want to get mixed up with. But it was raining and this fellow seemed like a nice guy. It was either climb in a warm bed with him and hope nothing happened or take my suitcase and look for a cheap motel.

We climbed into bed and the music man talked a little more about what a great salesman he was. Then I fell asleep.

I awoke with the music man's arm around me. He mumbled affectionately. I cringed, then realized my hugger was asleep. Perhaps a married man dreaming about his loving spouse. I gently lifted his arm to get free, then walked around the bed and climbed in. The rest of the night was blissful sleep.

Next morning the music man bought my breakfast and drove me to the bus line so I could reach the edge of town. He was such a nice man I almost hugged him.

Riding the bus created a problem. Rumors back home were that up north, black people would sit down right beside you. That was a disturbing thought so, seated on the bus, I sat my suitcase on the seat beside me with "Texas" there in big letters. No black person sat by me although several smiled and said "Good Morning." One black lady ignored the suitcase and told me which highway would take me toward Pennsylvania. It was a unique feeling to see the black folks walking on the sidewalks, not stepping aside for white folks, getting on the bus and choosing any seat they wanted, often right up front. It was like being on a different planet, not like what black folks had to do back home. On my next bus ride I put the suitcase on the floor where it belonged.

Meadville, Pennsylvania, was getting closer. Dropped off in a small town, I decided to part with a dime for a cold beer. Noisy blue collar men crowded the few tables in the bar. They paid little attention as I entered. Peanut hulls covered the floor, crunching under foot. A bowl of free peanuts welcomed me. I ordered a beer and sat alone at the bar, feeling lower than the proverbial snake's belly. Not much cash left, Meadville still a day away, and somebody else might already have that job. I sipped my beer in silence, tossing peanut shells on the floor like everybody else. Then I noticed a lone book on the back bar wall. A *Confidential List of Town Drunks*. That was intriguing. Finally I called the bartender over and whispered, "Could I see that book?"

He looked over his shoulder at his clients. All seemed to too busy to notice. "Okay," he whispered. "I'm not supposed to show it to strangers, but what the Hell."

I opened the book. My face looked back at me in the page size mirror. Behind me the bar rocked with laughter. I picked up my suitcase and headed for the highway.

Smoke on the Water

There may be a better way to get a job. But when a dusty applicant walked in carrying a suitcase after hitch hiking 1,500 miles, John Alden Cox of World Letters was impressed. "The job's still open," he said. "Our author, Desmond Holdridge, will go down through Mexico and South America. He'll write weekly letters and we need an assistant to mimeograph and mail them back here to fifteen hundred schools."

A little more time to get acquainted and the job was mine. Do well, get the author job next year. Sure there would be a next year. That war was three thousand miles away. And tonight we gather at the diner for the first full meal after days of hitchhiking. And it would be sleeping in a feather bed with no fat broads, reeking of beer, banging on the door.

Pay would be ten dollars a week and expenses. Equipment was a typewriter, mimeograph, addressograph with plates for the schools, enough mimeo stencils for the trip, and a camera with two lens. This was the type of camera used to make view cards for the Keystone View stereo kits. Two identical photos made with the two-eyed camera were printed side by side on a card. When seen through the viewer the photo appeared in three dimensions. Just like occasional movies made today which include special tinted glasses for 3-D viewing.

With briefing out of the way, visas were needed and that meant a quick trip to New York to visit consulates. Cox had gone to college with Lowell Thomas, radio newscaster who gained fame for vivid accounts about Lawrence of Arabia. "Let's see Lowell while we're here," Cox suggested.

An elevator zipped us far up a skyscraper to the studio. Thomas arrived a few minutes later. He had a brisk cleaned-with-a-toothbrush look and warm glad-to-know-you personality.

We sat in awe as he brought the nation up to date. When the news cast was over, Thomas pulled up a chair. "Now when you're down there in South America, call me if you run across a good story. Just pick up the phone and call collect." Then he brightened. "You are going to be in the Dominican Republic? Ciudad Trujillo? Great! On the outskirts of Ciudad Trujillo you'll find the ruins of the first church in the New World. I'm building a home out on Great Neck. The fireplace will be made of rocks from all over the world. While you are in Ciudad Trujillo, go out to the ruins and get me a rock." Glowing in new found importance, I promised to get that rock.

Back in Meadville there was one more test to pass. "The owners are concerned about sending you off on this long trip," my boss confided. "They want to know that you are dependable, that you won't go on a binge down there. So tonight they're having us over for dinner."

Then he grew serious. "They like to make Tom Collins. And they are going to serve 'em tonight. They will want to see how well you hold your liquor. Now those Tom Collins are really potent. Almost straight bourbon whiskey. So keep that in mind."

Sure enough, my new employers took great pride in their Tom Collins. Carefully crushed mint, bourbon just right, and glasses frosting on newspaper cushions in the refrigerators. And those Tom Collins were potent. So potent in fact that my bosses would never have qualified for the trip. As for me, I left cold sober.

Author Holdridge left early, heading down through Mexico. Thoroughly indoctrinated, properly warned of pitfalls including demon rum, I boarded the train to follow. The train ride would end at Brownsville. "We don't want you to go down through Mexico," my boss explained. "You need to be where you can easily get the supplies you need. You handle the Mexico letters from Brownsville. Just cross the river to Matamoros to buy stamps, then mail the letters in Mexico. That will take care of Mexico. Then you go to New Orleans to catch a boat. You'll spend three months in Caracas, then to Rio for three months, and finish in Buenos Aires." Tickets for complete trip from New Orleans South and then back to New York totaled three hundred and fifty dollars. Tourist class.

Compared to hitch hiking, that train ride South was first class. Sitting in the dining car, I could see hitch hikers standing on the highway. A few weeks before I had been out there too. Rolling across Texas, the train stopped for minutes in Bishop, my home town. No time to get off. Just sit at the open window and look down main street. Years growing up here flashed by in seconds. It was like a scene from *Our Town*. Those were long time friends out there, moving in a different world and no way to reach them. I wanted to yell, "Look, I'm back! Here on the train!" But they were all too far away, going about their business with never a look at the distant train chugging in the station. Then the conductor yelled "Board!" The train jerked forward and main street faded behind.

In Brownsville the job was easy. Type mimeograph stencils sitting on a breezy screened porch, print the letters, address envelopes, fold and stuff the letters. Then across the border to buy fifteen hundred stamps, back to Brownsville to stick 'em on, and back across the river to mail the letters in old Mexico. Whether the author wrote from Monterrey, Chiapas, or Mexico City it made no difference. That stamp was Mexico.

The war in Europe was far away. No one seemed to realize it was creeping a little closer. Just a hint came when young men were invited to take advantage of an unusual offer. Join the military for one year and that would be it. Hopefully by the time I returned there might not be any need for military service. With three thousand miles of surging salt water between us, we were not about to get involved. Let them fight their war.

First jingoistic hint came one evening in a Brownsville café. Diners paused now and then to get up and dance to the thump of a juke box. It was a happy scene until a new record dropped in place and the juke box blared again. A drunk angrily jumped to his feet. "All right you folks," he yelled. "Stand up! By God that is 'Smoke on the Water'!"

Nothing happened. Then a buddy yelled, "Aw George, that ain't the National Anthem."

"The Hell it ain't," the drunk answered, waving his arms. "That's 'Smoke on the Water' and you better stand up!"

Slowly diners rose and dancers stopped. All stood quietly while the juke box wailed:

THE GUNS NOBODY HEARD
23 YEARS THAT CHANGED AMERICA FOREVER

"There'll be smoke on the water
On the land and on the sea
When our Army and Navy
Overtake the enemy"

"Stand up! That is *'Smoke on the Water.'*"

When the song ended, diners sat down and dancers returned to their seats. All hoped the drunk would not put in another coin. If he did they would stand up again. That was the easy way. Don't get involved.

In Europe the same thing had happened. Hitler, their small time "drunk" had been ignored and now it was too late. There was smoke on the water, and it was blowing toward America.

To Catch a Spy

In New Orleans the *Westvangen* hoisted the gang plank and headed down the Mississippi. Her final destination would be Puerto Cabello, a Venezuelan port. From Puerto Cabello I would go overland to Caracas.

A small cargo ship, the *Westvangen* carried twelve passengers. An hour out the ship sailed smoothly along. Soon there was no sight of land, just endless water that stretched to the horizon. This was great. There would be no sea sickness here. Then the plump captain grinned and said, "No wonder the smooth sailing. We are still in the Mississippi."

My cabin mate was a young man from Ciudad Trujillo, our first port in the Dominican Republic. "When we get there," Carlos cautioned, "don't ever mention Trujillo's name. You will just get into trouble." His father, also on board, published the newspaper there. The father said nothing about Trujillo. The son, with the fervor of youth, was more outspoken. "Trujillo is a mean dictator. He is bad for my country. Kills his enemies and rules with an iron fist. We will have no peace until he is gone. You will see."

We docked and passengers went ashore to see this foreign port. At the plaza, loudspeakers mounted around the square blared the World Series in Spanish. Locals gathered in groups, following the play by play. A huge neon sign atop a two story building flashed, "Dios y Trujillo" (God and Trujillo). It was stupid but, in the arrogance of youth, I asked a local, "*Que es con este Señor Trujillo?*" (What about this Señor Trujillo?)

The local stiffened. "*No dice* " (*No dee cee.* Don't talk) he said and moved quickly away. He had ample reason. A rumor was that Dictator Trujillo had a mansion fronting the bay. A cut brought the water under the mansion. Dominicans who ran afoul of Trujillo were brought to the mansion, a trap door opened, and the rebel dropped into the water. Sharks moved in below.

With some time left before we sailed, I hailed a cab and was off to get that rock for Lowell Thomas. The ruins of the New World's first church were on a lonesome stretch of land not far from the ocean. Low walls, varying in height, outlined the ruins. In the distance, a lone soldier stood guard with bayoneted rifle. Rocks fallen from the low walls were scattered along the ground. I selected one that should look great with the other famous rocks in that fireplace. As I brushed off the dirt the guard hurried over. "No No," he ordered in Spanish, "You can not take anything from here."

I smiled. "Señor, you know of Lowell Thomas, the very famous radio news man back in North America?"

The soldier frowned, then brightened. "Oh yes."

"Well Señor, Mr. Thomas is going to build a fireplace in his home with rocks from famous buildings all over the world. He wants a rock from your famous building and he will tell everybody about it."

THE GUNS NOBODY HEARD
23 YEARS THAT CHANGED AMERICA FOREVER

The soldier smiled and nodded. "That would be nice. Take the rock!"

Then on to Venezuela. Life on board the *Westvangen* was pleasant. A few old books waited in the library but the good life was up on deck. The easy going captain welcomed passengers to the bridge to watch as he plotted the *Westvangen's* course. Up in the bow was a place to stand and watch porpoises racing alongside. Schools of flying fish leaped high above the waves. Now and then a loner sailed across the bow and splashed on the other side. "They fly well," the captain said, "but they are also very tasty broiled."

We docked at Puerto Cabello and I headed down the gang plank to find a taxi. As I came down the gang plank, natives gathered below and yelled in Spanish. "Get back on that ship. We don't want any damn Germans here."

Then I realized my sun toasted hair was now blonde with a Germanic look. "I'm no German," I yelled in Spanish. "I am *Americano*."

Angry frowns vanished. "*Bueno!* We like Americans."

For the first time the far off war was brought closer. Clearing the "welcome" group, I found a taxi ready to make the twenty-five mile trip to Caracas. Bags loaded we followed the narrow road through sugar cane fields. Then the driver slowed and stopped. A large group of natives, each carrying a machete, gathered around a low walled square. "You should see this." The driver grinned.

Inside the arena, two bloody roosters glared at each other, then slammed together.

They wore *espuelas*, sharp metal spikes, on each leg. They collided again and again as natives yelled encouragement. Another hit and the larger rooster staggered, then collapsed in a bloody heap. The survivor swerved, ready to strike again, then crowed in victory. Winners laughed as they gathered pesos from machete carrying losers. I nudged the driver. "This place might explode. Let's get out of here."

"Get back on that ship. We don't want any damn Germans here."

THE GUNS NOBODY HEARD
23 YEARS THAT CHANGED AMERICA FOREVER

"No Señor." The driver grinned. "The *trabajadores* they don't fight like the roosters. They watch a little while, make the bets, and go back to cutting the cane."

Caracas was peaceful. No war talk here. Downtown was typical Spanish. A statue of Simon Bolivar reigned in the square. This was sacred ground and no one was allowed here without a coat. Clever natives, too poor to own a coat, came to the square wearing pajama tops. Another way to beat the local fuzz.

Taxis passing the hotel flashed "*Libre*" signs. That had to be a local term for "Taxi." When time came to go get postage stamps I telephoned and asked for a libre. The person answering said, "*No entiende,*" which meant, "I don't understand." Disgusted I asked a local how to reach the libre people. "*Libre* does not mean taxi. It means 'free.' There is no passenger in the cab." Another call, this time for a "taxi," and we were off to buy stamps.

Asked for fifteen hundred stamps, the postal clerk shook his head and pointed to a doorway. This was the office of the Postmaster General of Venezuela. The General, a young man of about thirty five, sat behind a huge desk. "Why," he asked, "do you want fifteen hundred stamps?" He listened politely, made a telephone call, and in minutes a clerk came in with the stamps. Each week I bought my stamps from the Postmaster General of Venezuela.

Caracas in 1940 had narrow streets. Drivers sped along these streets and squeezed a rubber ball powered horn at each blind corner. The horns were attached to the steering wheel. Squeezing the rubber ball sent a high pitched blast. Approaching a corner at a fast clip, a driver squeezed off one screech. If an answering blast came from the right, the driver stopped. If the answer came from the left the first honker had

25

the right of way. You can imagine the honking that erupted at each blind intersection. Amazingly there were few accidents. When a collision happened drivers jumped out and ran away. Unless caught immediately they were home free. Any injured person was to be left until the ambulance arrived.

Soon it was time to leave and head for Rio de Janeiro. The twenty five miles of highway down the mountain from Caracas to La Guira was a tortuous, twisting drive. It took the taxi two and a half hours to reach the port. My ship, the Japanese *Seia Maru*, was late. No hotel in La Guira so back up that twisting mountain road for another two and a half hours.

Back down the next day and there was the *Seia Maru*. The captain waited at the gang plank. "I'm sorry," he said, "but I am not going to Rio de Janeiro. We have a damaged propeller and must go back to Cristobal."

Now I had a problem. My boss back in Meadville had covered all the bases except for a damaged propeller. Now I suddenly had to make my own travel plans or stay stuck in Caracas.

The harbor master helped. "There's a Dutch ship leaving tonight for Trinidad and Barbados," he said. "The *U.S.S. Argentina* stops at Barbados on the sixteenth, then goes on to Rio."

That was great news. Now to let my boss know. The telegraph operator shook his head, "No, you can't send that message. There's a war going on." So I let the boss simmer when he found out I would be in Barbados.

The Dutch ship carried cargo and passengers. My roommate was Carlos Schneider, a young German who had also been booked on the *Seia Maru*. We met in the cabin just as the ship began moving. "You better close those port holes," Schneider suggested.

"Why do that?" I asked, and noticed that the backside of the port hole cover was black.

"Because the Dutch are at war with Germany," my cabin mate explained.

War? We could get torpedoed. I wanted out, and fast. But no luck. The harbor was behind us.

We made it through the night, stopped for a short time at Trinidad, and then on to Barbados. There the war would get even closer.

The ship anchored outside the harbor. No facilities for docking here. It was raining and the tender that waited had canvas side flaps lowered. We climbed aboard and the launch headed for the dock. As we chugged along Schneider, seated a couple of places down and backed by the canvas flaps, tore up some papers. With the flap behind him, Carlos could not drop the scraps into the water. He leaned to reach me. "Will you toss these for me?" he asked. As I took the papers a sailor across the aisle jerked forward, then dropped back into his seat. I dropped the paper scraps into the roiling water.

The next morning I went back to the dock to check in with Barbados police. When the finger printing was done, the brisk sergeant said, "Captain Weymss wants to see you."

The captain was a smartly unformed young man of probably twenty-five. Later we learned his father commanded an army in Africa. "Welcome to Barbados," the captain said, and then became serious. "What did you take from Mr. Schneider in the launch yesterday and throw overboard?"

"I'm sorry, Sir," I replied, "but I don't remember taking anything from Mr. Schneider."

The captain shouted an order and a young sailor entered. He snapped to rigid attention. "Corporal," the captain began, "did you see this gentleman on the launch yesterday?"

"Yes, Sir!" the corporal answered. "He took some papers from Mr. Schneider and threw them in the water."

Now it came back. "You are right," I confessed. "I forgot all about it. Just some scraps."

"Perhaps," the captain said sternly. "You may go to your hotel but come back here tomorrow morning. By then we will have a better idea who you are. You say you are traveling through South America sending back letters. You could be a courier. We will know by tomorrow."

Now, suddenly, the war was here. This was an island, there was no escape, and the British were in command. If they decided I was a spy that could mean a firing squad. Far fetched but who knew what wrong reports, if any, the captain might get. It was a troubled and restless night.

The next morning the captain was more relaxed. "You check out okay," he began. "We have been in touch with your consulate in Caracas. Now I would like to ask a favor."

"Of course," I answered quickly, glad to be off his spy list.

"Your country is not at war," the captain continued. "But your country does favor us, your British cousins. We think Schneider is a German courier. But we have to know for sure. There will be a dance at the Yacht Club next Saturday night. Suppose I get a date for you and then you can tell Schneider you also have a date for him. His date will be one of our operatives."

Again, "of course" was the only answer. This was a British island and I was stuck there until the *Argentina* came through. If it turned out Mr. Schneider danced to a different drummer that would be too bad.

Cinderella had more time to get ready for the ball. But the British were speedy. A local tailor said he could have a jacket ready by Saturday morning. One fitting would do. Tux pants and other needed trappings were already available. Meanwhile unsuspecting Carlos was delighted to hear he had a date for the dance. We would go together.

The linen jacket, tailor made to snugly fit, was ready Saturday morning. The cost, in U.S., was ten dollars. Tux pants cost eleven dollars. Saturday evening, feeling dapper in the handsome linen jacket and tux pants, I reported for final instructions. Captain H. Colchester Weymss took me in at a glance, then exclaimed "I say, old chap. You can't go to the ball in *white* shoes!"

"I'm sorry, Sir. These are all I have."

The captain shrugged. "All right then, let's see what we can do." He led the way to a closet and opened the door. A row of impeccable shoes filled the closet floor. "Try on some of these," he ordered. "One pair should fit you."

We finally found a pair for a very tight fit. "These will do," the captain announced. "They are a bit tight, old chap, and may hurt a while. But after a couple of drinks you won't feel them at all." He was right.

My date was an attractive young British girl. The captain quite properly took me by her house. Her parents welcomed us, ready to send their daughter and car off with a stranger if it would help the Crown. Schneider's date was a stunning red head. She got Schneider so drunk he was a talking, rambling bore. What his rambling revealed is still a mystery. When the *Argentina* sailed for Rio Schneider was not on it.

For the people in Barbados, the war was here.

A War Beyond a War

The U.S.S. *Argentina* sailed from Barbados on December 16, 1940. Pearl Harbor was less than a year away. No one on board seemed concerned, except a lusty young Italian woman. She held court in the bar, loudly extolling the virtues of Mussolini. "A great man!" she insisted. "A great man who will lead Italy to new heights."

There was a grim reminder war could come near, if only by mistake. Twin American flags flew at the stern. At night searchlights lit the stern and twin Stars and Stripes to warn German submarines this was a U.S. Ship. Two years later a German submarine would sink this same ship on a trip back to New York. But for now life aboard ship was pleasant. lolling on the deck in the warm sunlight or joining in dance lessons led by the happy cruise director. Band members, working late, went for a swim after work and then stretched by the pool for a nap. The next morning they awoke terribly blistered. This was the equator and the sun was unforgiving.

THE GUNS NOBODY HEARD
23 YEARS THAT CHANGED AMERICA FOREVER

Dark cliffs heralded the approach of Brazil. Then Sugar Loaf loomed. As we entered the harbor we passed three German freighters. Sailors, happily interned for the rest of the war, waved as we passed.

At Customs, the agent flipped open baggage and rattled Portuguese. I replied in Spanish. Each of us understood a little but not enough. It was time to display a letter of introduction from the Pan American Union. In Spanish, the letter extolled the virtues of World Letters, stressed flow of good will to U.S. schools. This service would, the letter glowed, promote "International Citizenship." Great words but wrong place.

The agent brightened. "Oh yes," he said in Portuguese and wrote rapidly on a pad. "Tomorrow you go to this address and they will fix it so you can come and get your baggage." In Portuguese that was "bah gah gee" but it sounded great to me. With fifteen hundred letters to print and mail, I urgently needed my "bah gah gee."

The address was a lovely Villa on the outskirts of Rio. Inside chairs lined a long wall. Each was filled with someone waiting to go through a distant office door. I waited all day, moving from chair to chair, and never reached the door.

That night at the rooming house I protested loudly, lamenting the long and frustrating delay and still no "bah gah gee."

"What are you doing out there?" an Embassy employee asked.

He listened and announced, "Tomorrow I will go out there with you."

The row of chairs was waiting but my friend stormed past and into the office. Moments later he came out and said, "Come on, let's go get your baggage."

"Why did they make me wait?" I asked.

"You won't believe this," he laughed. "They thought you wanted to be a citizen. They were getting your papers ready."

Once the "bah gah gee" was in hand, work in Rio was fantastic. While the author trekked through steaming jungles his assistant worked until five, then hit the surf. Copacobana beach stretched in a beautiful curve. A wide mosaic sidewalk separated street and sand. The water was clean and warm. Waves started gently far out, then surged larger and swept smoothly to the beach. Perfect for body surfing. No sharks here. Only a giant manta ray who, just beyond our depth, soared out of the water and pancaked in a huge belly buster.

The work place was just as great. The *pension*, as boarding houses were called, was owned by a British couple. It was a block from Copacobana beach. Room and board, with morning and afternoon tea, was thirty five dollars American. The mimeograph whirled, letters flowed, and a young Brazilian who loved the money helped get the 1,500 letters stamped and in the mail each week.

Swim time was after five and then back to the basement shower. There a parrot watched from nearby and occasionally rattled Portuguese. He was a challenge, and an opportunity for some fun. After each afternoon swim, it was time for the parrot's lesson. "Heil Hitler!" called out time after time, began to sink in. Soon the parrot said it perfectly. When it came time to leave for Buenos Aires, it was good to know the British couple were in for a surprise.

Approaching Montevideo the war suddenly loomed close again. The super structure of the *Graf Spee* rose grotesquely above the waves. A silent reminder that here a great warship had gone down, sunk by her captain who in stark tradition went down with her.

THE GUNS NOBODY HEARD
23 YEARS THAT CHANGED AMERICA FOREVER

Then on to Buenos Aires. In many ways reminiscent of a great city like Boston, Buenos Aires seemed placid at first glance. This was far from the truth. Large colonies of British and Germans faced each other in this neutral land. Anger seethed below the surface and often erupted at night. An overturned van flamed in the street or a German or a British doorway was smashed. In one theater newsreel, German fighters sent British planes down in flames while the audience cheered. In another, British Spitfires blasted German bombers as shouts of approval rocked the theater.

Back in Barbados, Schneider had given me a Buenos Aires phone number. "If I get out of here I'll be in Buenos Aires. Call me when you get there later this year." So I dialed the number and a gruff voice answered. "May I speak to Mr. Schneider?"

"He is not here!" and the phone slammed down.

When final letters were mailed it was time to head back for America. That one year of service young men had rushed to sign, had suddenly been replaced by the draft. A German woman urged, "Don't go back. You'll be drafted. They don't care about you. They'll send you off to kill or be killed. Stay here!" She was doing her bit for the Fuhrer.

There is a strange feeling when you are alone in a foreign land and your homeland is at war or on the verge. Even though a draft waits, you want to go home. That feeling could be the difference between life and death but it was there.

The time was May, 1941 and the ship was again the *U.S.S. Argentina*. A warm welcome from the stewards and bartenders and sad news about the Italian girl. "One of our stewards was a British agent," a crew member revealed. "He courted her a bit, got into her cabin, and found letters under her mattress. The British took her off at Trinidad and shot her." So much for Mussolini's ardent booster. Thinking of her, one wondered if Schneider met the same fate.

On the return lighted flags again flew on the stern. But the feeling aboard was far different. Perhaps it was because Jewish refugees now crowded the tourist section. Sad, grim people, they had escaped the Nazis. Too short on funds for first class, they traveled in tourist.

THE GUNS NOBODY HEARD
23 YEARS THAT CHANGED AMERICA FOREVER

My cabin mate was fleeing with his mother. Their small country was captured by the Russians. His father, not so fortunate, had been the President. Memory fades with time. The country may have been Lithuania.

At last a giant torch emerged on the horizon. Slowly the Statue of Liberty rose from the sea. It was May 1941 and we were coming home. Passengers cheered and refugees embraced each other as the New York harbor neared.

My boss met me at the dock. "I'm sorry," he began, "but there will be no trip next year with you as author. Travel is too hard. Arrangements too unpredictable." As we looked back at passengers streaming off the ship, he grinned. "This dock has memories for me. I came back from World War One right here. I was a second lieutenant and in charge of bales of blue denims stacked on the deck. As we docked a colonel nabbed me and told me to go down on the dock and find a major. I protested, telling him I was in charge of the bales of denim. That didn't matter. He ordered me to go. When I got back on deck, the denims were gone. They had been hoisted off the deck, loaded on trucks, and long gone. So I said to hell with it and walked up to Broadway and out of the Army."

Then he laughed. "Just a week ago I got a letter from the War Department wanting to know what happened to those blue denims. I'll get it straightened out, but damn, this is twenty three years later!"

Before heading back to Texas, a trip to the draft office was in order. The man was nice and sympathetic. "Son, your number has already been called. But we'll give you a month to get things in order."

Back in Texas military camps were popping up. In the news, President Roosevelt had given four over age destroyers to the British. No one explained what "over age" meant. Those were fighting ships. The key words, which lulled us into unconcern, were "over age." America was moving toward war but no one seemed to sense it. A sort of malaise was across the land. It wasn't economic. The Depression was slowly ebbing, powered by the surge in military spending. Yet the public was oblivious to steady preparations of war. The camps and draft were merely a way to keep the nation safe. The war was three thousand miles away, far across a protective moat. We were not about to get in that far off "Idiot's Delight" as playwright Robert Sherwood called it.

Next a trip to the doctor for a draft physical. The office was on Austin's South Congress, near the railroad tracks, and the day was hot. The brisk doctor asked questions, thumped my chest a couple of times, then stuck a needle in my arm to draw blood.

I fainted.

When I awakened, I apologized. "I'm sorry, Doctor," I said, thinking this weakness and the sight of blood made me unfit. "I wanted to serve my country."

The doctor moved in front of the chair to face me. "Son," he announced, up close and personal, "You are IN!"

On the nearby track a passenger train moved slowly past the doctor's office. As it picked up speed the chug chug of the drivers seemed to say, "I'll be back for you."

Panic in the Afternoon

The clippers buzzed and hair tumbled to the floor in clumps. For young men there can be nothing more debilitating. One after another, Marine recruits climbed into the barber's chair. Anyone could do the barbering. Start at the back, then push the buzzing clipper across the scalp. It was like shearing a sheep but this time the sheep were Marines. Well almost. We were "boots," the lowest form of life on a Marine Corps base.

The sergeant in charge grinned smugly as shorn recruits waited for the last to be sheared. Then he marched us back to long tent rows to begin boot camp at Recruit Depot, San Diego. Tents had rough wooden floors and four cots. Each boot, as recruits were called, had a foot locker beneath his cot and that ended the amenities.

Life was going to be different. All personal rights vanished with our hair. Returning from a day of marching, one exhausted Marine knelt to unlock his foot locker. He groped for his keys.

No keys. "Don't worry," a buddy offered, "you probably left them in the lock and the sergeant picked them up. He checks tents while we're gone. Go ask him."

The boot walked down the sandy tent row to the sergeant's tent. He knocked on the tent pole. That seemed stupid since the sergeant was clearly visible, sitting on his cot. But orders were orders. "Sir, Private Rogers requests permission to speak to the sergeant."

"Certainly, Private Rogers. What can I do for you?"

"Sir, I think I left my keys in my locker. They said maybe you picked them up on your rounds."

The sergeant brought a box of keys. "I probably did, Private Rogers. I've got a lot of keys."

The boot grinned. "Yes, Sir, and these are mine." He reached for a set of keys but the sergeant's big hand intervened.

"Hold on, Private Rogers. We can't be sure those are your keys."

"But, Sir, I know my keys."

"We need to be sure, Private Rogers. So you just bring your locker and we'll make sure. And, Private Rogers, bring it by yourself."

The recruit's tent was at least a hundred feet from the sergeant's. The foot locker was bulky and heavy. Rogers staggered down the tent row. The sergeant pushed a key into the lock, turned it, and smiled. "You're right, Private Rogers. These are your keys."

"Thank you, Sir," Rogers gasped.

"Certainly, Private Rogers. Glad to help anytime."

Rogers stumbled back to his tent, carrying a foot locker that never again would be left with keys dangling.

They may call it "boot camp" because boots bang the sand from dawn until late afternoon. Sergeant Chadwick and

THE GUNS NOBODY HEARD
23 YEARS THAT CHANGED AMERICA FOREVER

Corporal Cleland marched our platoon across the sand dunes chanting, "Your left, two, three four, your left two three four." From the nearby airfield two Ryan monoplanes rose from the runway. As a plane climbed the instructor pulled back the throttle. He was training his student to quickly slam the nose over if the engine failed. Get the nose over quickly to prevent a stall and crash

When a climbing plane suddenly dipped downward, our sergeant yelled, "Air raid! Air raid!" The platoon hit the sand face down. Lying on the hot sand I thought, "What am I doing lying here when I could be up there?"

So I wrote a letter to the Commandant, Naval Air Station, Pensacola. "I am twenty-three years old, have a college degree, in excellent health and I want to fly for the Navy." Stick on a three cent stamp and drop the letter in the mail box at the end of tent row. It was a gesture, a futile attempt to break through the tangle of bureaucracy. Pigs would fly before I did.

One day the marching was halted so a sergeant could address gathered platoons. "The Corps is going to grow real quick," he promised. "You guys are privates now but you are gonna have a chance to make sergeant in four years. It took me ten years." No one thought about the reason for this sudden growth. That war was far away.

Boot camp ended. Orders came for the platoon. Most went to the infantry. Several of us were assigned to Sea School. Here Marines were trained for duty aboard ship. "You're going to the *Boise* as clerk for the Marines," Sergeant Miller told me. "And you'll be a member of a five inch gun crew."

The *Boise* was a heavy cruiser, destined to take heavy damage in the Battle of the Coral Sea. Although there were rumors the Japanese were becoming an annoyance in the Pacific Rim, Sergeant Miller pooh poohed that. Sea duty, he promised, would be a cake walk. "I served on the *Texas* and we watched Jap battle units at target practice. They couldn't hit the proverbial bull in the butt with a bass fiddle. No wonder. Most Japs have weak eyes. They wear glasses that look like the bottom of coke bottles."

It didn't occur that Sergeant Miller, like the rest of us, formed his optical opinion watching Japanese pilots in the movies. They were always bad guys, wearing thick glasses on their mean little noses.

Marine drill sergeants had a fantastic knack for punishing all members of a platoon when one goofed. Thanksgiving, 1941, provided a good example. Food was always great and the Thanksgiving spread was fantastic. Huge platters of turkey and dressing for each eight man table. "There's just one catch," the sergeant announced as kitchen duty Marines lugged in the platters. "You guys get all the turkey you want *after* you eat the dressing."

That seemed fair so we dug in. Soon the turkey was gone at one table, and oh joyous news, so was the dressing! More turkey for those guys while us turkey less Marines still faced a platter filled with dressing.

Dinner over, we marched back to the barrack and flopped on cots. This would be a wonderful afternoon with no marching. Then the mess sergeant knocked on our sergeant's door.

They talked in low voices. Then our sergeant called attention. "Some of you guys dumped dressing under the table so you could get more turkey. Okay, who did it?"

Total silence. A Marine did not rat on a fellow marine.

The sergeant shrugged. "Nobody talking? Okay, get your rifles and back packs and get your over stuffed butts outside!"

Groans echoed down the row of cots. Slowly the groggy

group fetched rifles and back packs. Sergeant Miller was waiting out on the concrete with his rifle and back pack. "Rifles at high port," he ordered, "and keep up with me. Let's go!"

Turkey stuffed Marines followed him down the long parade ground. Several dropped to the pavement up chucking. Still Miller kept going at a fast trot. Reaching the far end, he turned and led staggering remnants back to the barrack. He entered his office, returned his rifle to the overhead rack, stretched on his cot and resumed reading his pulp magazine. Other less fit Marines staggered to their bunks and collapsed.

One morning movie actors John Payne and Randolph Scott arrived to "case" the area for upcoming action in *The Shores of Tripoli*. Our company would march in a stirring scene while John Payne, surrounded by marching Marines, would strip off civilian clothes and change into the Marine uniform.

Sergeant Miller faced the company before filming began. He called me out of ranks. "What Congressman or Senator do you know?" the Sergeant demanded.

"Sir, I don't know anybody."

"Then how come you are getting orders to flight school?"

Hot damn, I was out of here! No more flopping in the sand when an airplane dived. Now I would be up there where it is cool.

"Fall out," the Sergeant ordered. I stepped from ranks. "Private, no use you being in the front rank when they start filming and then drop out. And since you are going to be an officer you had better know what us enlisted men put up with. Starting right now you will be in charge of the head detail."

The head detail each day consisted of Marines with various minor ailments. Although in sick bay they were well enough to police the grounds and also clean the large restrooms. "So get at it," the sergeant ordered, "and get those restrooms ready for inspection."

That was no easy task. I had no rank to pull on sick bay Marines. They cleaned as much as they felt like doing. The rest was up to me. It was a grinding two weeks until orders came to head for Long Beach. The Navy was not yet into the language where a short person is described as "vertically challenged." The Navy was blunt. The outfit that waited was the "Elimination Base." It was a place you went to be eliminated.

Flight training was at Long Beach municipal airport. Twice a day an airline DC-3 landed and took off. Otherwise the field belonged to the Navy aircraft. These were twin cockpit fabric covered biplanes. Top speed was about 90 knots.

My instructor was a Marine major who did not want his fellow Marine eliminated. He worked hard and answered lots of questions. Example, "What do you do if the engine quits?"

"Push the nose down to keep air speed. Don't make any big turns or you are liable to stall and spin in. Just glide straight ahead."

"What if there are trees?"

"Go between them. Let 'em take off the wings but don't turn."

His instruction was life saving. On a crisp December morning I practiced turns at 4,000 feet, throttled back to glide down to a thousand, then climbed back upstairs. Gliding down on the second series, I rolled out of a turn and shoved the throttle forward. *Kerpow!* The prop slowed, then stopped. Get the nose down! Hold the stick tight in sweaty hands. Keep that airspeed at 65 knots, wings level. Trees up ahead. Clear them or go between. Now over the trees and *Hallelujah!* A practice pasture was straight ahead! But there's a fence. She's still flying and, wonder of wonders, over the fence and bumpety bump. The N3N rolled to a stop. Dead stick landing!

Someone reported the landing. Soon another N3N arrived. The officer took in the situation at a glance. "Carburetor froze," he announced. "The temperature is lower up there. And there's a lot of moisture in the air. You need to put on carburetor heat in those gliding turns." He sat in the cockpit while I stood on the lower wing and cranked the starter. The engine kicked over, caught, and in no time I was headed for the airport.

The first Sunday in December arrived. It was my day for guard duty. That meant four hours out on the airport boundary, standing at ease with rifle on shoulder or pacing slowly back and forth.

Suddenly something happened at the distant hangars. People ran across the tarmac. An officer raced to a trainer. A chief ran with him, carrying a sub machine gun. They took off and headed for the ocean.

Finally a replacement showed up. "Pearl Harbor's been bombed!"

Panic was everywhere. The plane with the sub machine gun was headed for an outlying field near the ocean. The mission? To stop the Japanese. They were bound to be coming in.

At dusk the rain pelted in a steady downpour. The lieutenant in charge sent for me. "You're a Marine and you know about combat," he began. "Come with me to check the sentries. We're at war! Those Japs could be hitting the beach!" He was obviously all shook up and he wasn't alone. We walked down the narrow passageway between barracks. Yellow lights flickered in the rain. To our right a student sentry advanced, rifle at port. And to our left another approached, rifle ready.

"Who goes there?" one yelled, his rifle aimed at the other.

"Who goes there?" the second sentry yelled, his rifle ready.

"Dammit, I asked you first!"

The lieutenant charged into the clearing. "Back off! Lower those rifles! Garner, you challenged first. So Shulz, you are supposed to answer."

"Yes, Sir," Shulz answered. "Flight student Shulz!"

"Well come on ahead then."

The lieutenant sloshed through the mud to face Garner. "Dammit Garner, you are supposed to say 'Proceed and be recognized'!"

"I'm sorry, Sir. All right, Shulz, proceed and be recognized."

Shulz sloshed through the mud and faced Garner.

"Well you sure are Shulz!" Garner exclaimed. He turned to the lieutenant. "Sir, did I get it right?" The lieutenant nodded grimly.

The same night a torpedo missed its target and slammed up on the sand at Long Beach, California. The Japanese were out there beyond the breakers.

Island in the Storm

Drive South of Corpus Christi along the bay front, past Ward Island where something strange called Radar was going on, and armed sailors stopped you at the entrance to the Naval Air Station. Here in a secluded area far from the wars that raged in Europe and the Pacific, the Navy trained hundreds of young men to fly airplanes in those far off wars. Escaping elimination at Long Beach, we arrived at Corpus Christi eager to earn our Navy Wings.

The time was February, 1942, and those far off wars were not going well. But here airplanes waited to be flown. It was easy at first. A repeat of Long Beach, with ten more hours of instruction just to refresh lagging memories. Then into six months of training to win our wings and a ticket to the war.

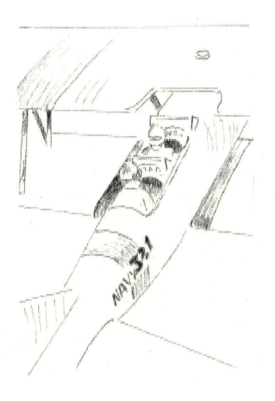

Now we trained in Stearman "Yellow Peril" biplanes. These were twin cockpit fabric covered planes with a top speed very close to that of the fighters that flew in World War I. The instructor sat in the front cockpit, partially under the overhanging top wing. The gas tank was in the top wing, a grim reminder to keep this crate right side up. Communication was primitive. It depended on a "gosport." This was a flexible metal tube. The instructor's end had a canvas flap to cover his mouth and block outside noises. The tube was passed back to the student and plugged into his helmet. The instructor's voice was distant and muffled, like speech through a pipe.

Most of us could follow the muffled instructions. One who failed was Marlowe, an ensign who came from the fleet and gave up his commission to get Navy wings. Marlowe did great in the normal routines. He flew well. Then aerobatics came along. When his instructor's piped voice ordered, "Gimme a right snap roll," Marlowe snapped to the left. After a number of foul ups, the instructor ordered a hearing check. The destroyer's guns had taken their toll. Marlowe's hearing was impaired. He went back to the fleet.

To cadets involved in the struggle to pass ground school and precise flying, the war was far away. Perhaps it was a form of denial. Don't think about what the future might hold but handle the present. Cold reality hit when an instructor happened to caution, "Don't skid in those turns. Before long your airplane will be a gun platform. If you skid in turns you can't hit a Jap. Miss your shot and you could be a dead duck."

Reality hit also when fighter pilots came back from the far Pacific. There was Lieutenant Thatch, a quiet business-like man. He might have been an engineer or an inventor, which he was when it came to fighter tactics. Thatch was the inventor of the "Thatch Weave," a maneuver saving pilot lives as they battled Zeros. Using his hands, Lt. Thatch showed how two fighter pilots now slid from side to side for joint protection.

There were bits of fun to break the grim routine. A cadet we'll call Fred in case he is still among us, announced "Tomorrow I am going to San Antonio." That Texas city was 150 miles Northwest and far outside our practice areas. "No sweat," Fred confided. "I'll just get lost and follow the highway to Randolph Field."

The next afternoon when flying was completed and we

boarded the bus, Fred was not among us. He was in far off San Antonio, his "Yellow Peril" parked alongside the Air Forces fighters and bombers. There no one knew the exact standing of a Navy cadet. Fred was treated as an officer until a pilot arrived from Corpus and ordered him into the back seat. Fred came home a grinning hero who proved you could have a bit of fun and get away with it.

On another more tragic day, two planes crashed on the field. Ordered not to land, trainers circled. Now we had radios and one callous circler used his. "Dr. Brent, call surgery. Dr. Brent, call surgery."

For some, gold wings never came. Our last flight before graduation was "gunnery" practice out over the Gulf. No bullets to fire, just diving runs at a towed target. We flew in stacked echelon. When the target approached the lead plane swung away in a steep dive at the target. Then the next plane flashed away.

As we waited our turn a plane lagged back in the formation, then rose abruptly. The plane above it shuddered as a propeller, like a giant buzz saw, ripped into the fuselage. As the crippled plane dropped, the pilot released his seat belt. He floated upward, high above the falling plane, still grabbing where the seat belt release had been. Then his parachute opened.

A cadet was still in the canopy covered back cockpit. "Bail out, bail out!" we yelled as the crippled plane plummeted. At four hundred feet a flash of white and the parachute popped open.

The plane hit the water. Above, the swaying parachute settled gently into the Gulf. "I tried to slide back the canopy," the cadet said later. "Then as I reached down to release my seat belt the canopy slammed shut. Finally I snapped loose the seat belt and then opened the canopy." Another hundred feet and it would have been too late.

THE GUNS NOBODY HEARD
23 YEARS THAT CHANGED AMERICA FOREVER

First thought was the pilot who did the damage would be blamed. The brass saw it differently. Flying in formation, a pilot had to hold position on the plane below. So after his harrowing escape, the pilot of the damaged plane was "washed out."

Tickets to the War

Pinning on the Navy's gold wings was done with mixed emotions. Cadet days, protected from the guns of war, were over. For most the wings were a ticket to the war that raged in the Pacific. A few of us went to instructor's school. This would delay combat a year or two.

A month in instructor's school, learning to keep up a line of patter as we flew, and it was off to a primary station. Mine was Dallas, another "island" with the war blocked off and far away. This became evident on the first trip to town. "Come and see us at the Adolphus," fellow instructor Bud urged. He and wealthy friend Willie spurned Bachelor Officers Quarters and had rooms at the Adolphus. After a day of flying, they went home to the whirl of Dallas night life.

Just as I entered the lobby here came Bud and Willie, headed for action. "Come on," Bud said and waved, "we are going to Abe and Pappy's." He hailed a cab.

It slid to the curb and the driver welcomed, "Where to, gentlemen?"

"Abe and Pappy's," Bud ordered.

The driver spun in his seat. "Where did you say?"

"Abe and Pappy's," Bud repeated as he closed the door.

The driver shrugged. "Okay, whatever you say." He shifted into gear, pulled away from the curb, and angled across the street. He slid to a stop at the curb and announced, "Abe and Pappy's!"

Bud paid the charge, adding a generous tip, and we headed up the stairs to Abe and Pappy's. The nightclub rocked with hilarity. Beer flowed but revelers brought scotch or bourbon in paper sacks. This was the law. Abe and Pappy's had a cover charge but cash flow came from ice and mixers. Sacks with bourbon, scotch, vodka and gin were stashed under the table and brought up when drinks were poured. Strange carrying on but this was the law. At midnight dancing continued but ice and mixer service stopped. This also stopped drinking unless revelers wisely stocked ice and mixers in advance.

Each night downtown Dallas was an island of revelry. Lou Ann's, a night club out on the fringe with an open air dance floor, was also packed every night. The beat went on and the revelers, as they mixed their drinks and danced the night away, knew the war was out there waiting for each of them.

"Fats" Ewing, who was not fat but solid muscle, filled a cockpit. He called civilian men sand crabs. "They run and hide in holes," he said disdainfully. At Abe and Pappy's, Fats and a buddy carried this disdain too far. They blocked the door to the men's restroom. "No sand crabs coming in here," Fats yelled. Fists flew and then Abe, or maybe it was Pappy, broke it up. Fat's "sand crabs" were not avoiding the war. Most of them were workers at the aircraft factories between Dallas and Fort Worth.

In contrast one clever man in Dallas was evading the war. A trim Air Force Lieutenant Colonel, he charmed a lonely, gullible lady. Could he leave his suit bag in her closet while he carried out his orders in the Dallas area? She readily agreed. The officer took her dancing in the evening and was busy in the daytime. After several days, she happened to open the closet. The bulky suit bag nudged her curiosity. She decided to sneak a peak at his other military uniforms and slid down the zipper. She stared in amazement. Lieutenant Colonels didn't wear blue uniforms with two and a half gold stripes on the sleeve. That would be a Navy Lieutenant Commander. She probed deeper. A second uniform was for an Army Major, not an Air Force Lieutenant Colonel. Two more impeccable uniforms provided the "officer" with neat changes. Like Super Man all he needed was a phone booth.

The amazed woman called the F.B.I. When the "Lieutenant Colonel" returned from a day of Dallas "duty" the Feds welcomed him. Now the closet was bare and the lady was sadder but wiser.

Since the Adolphus and Baker Hotels had higher cover charges, few enlisted men joined the dancers. The Adolphus had a dance floor that, at show time, slid back to reveal an ice rink. Dot Franey and her dancers whizzed out on the ice. Across Akard Street, the Baker Hotel had no ice rink but it had the Mural Room and a great band. Dance there and you might bump into flight student Robert Taylor if wife Barbara Stanwyck was visiting.

When Taylor joined the Navy he was the leading heart throb on the silver screen. His flight instructor, "Red Horse" Myers wondered just how Taylor would wow the women in his Navy khakis. Red Horse was driving with his student in Dallas one evening. They stopped at a traffic light just as a bevy of girls waited to cross. "Speak to 'em, Bob," Red Horse urged. Complying Taylor smiled and said, "Hello Ladies. How are you?" The women turned abruptly away and headed across the street. Perhaps the wise guy looked a bit like Robert Taylor but he sure was not Robert Taylor.

The 'Down' Patrol

While the beat went on each night in Dallas, flying began at the crack of dawn fifteen miles away at Grand Prairie. Two large circular mats served as runways. Instructors and their students, intermingled with lone students, zigzagged out to the mats to start the day. In the tower above the hangar, an Aldis lamp flashed. Green, you're cleared for take off. Red, hold your position. When the Yellow Perils returned in a wide sweeping gaggle an hour and a half later, no light flashed. Only a red light to send some goof ball around.

Too many planes coming in at once. Just watch your back and set 'er down. Accidents happened. A lone student probably returning from his first solo practice, landed on top of another. The propeller ripped into the plane below. One cadet died. The other "washed out" and went back to the fleet. He would carry the tragedy the rest of his life. His instructor suffered also. He made a mistake and sent the wrong student out alone.

THE GUNS NOBODY HEARD
23 YEARS THAT CHANGED AMERICA FOREVER

New instructors reporting for duty got a familiarization ride around the area. My pilot was a fast talking and openly self confident lieutenant. He climbed in the front cockpit and passed back the gosport. I hooked the flexible tube to my student helmet and we were off.

My tour guide described area boundaries as we left the field. Then we were over the practice area, flying at a thousand feet. Suddenly he slammed the plane into an inverted snap roll.

It spun violently with us thrown against seat belts. Back in level flight, I seethed with anger. This man, at low altitude, had foolishly risked our lives in a maneuver that could kill us both. But he was a senior lieutenant and I was an ensign. I seethed in silence.

A week later the same lieutenant took a student along the same route as they headed for the practice area. Flying at a thousand feet, he again kicked full rudder and slammed the stick forward in his prized maneuver. The airplane spun half around. Unable to recover at the low altitude the pilot and his student crashed to their deaths.

We went to his funeral. Naval aviators don't cry. We held back sobs when an officer handed a folded flag to the wife and four year old daughter. Except for a spin that went well, I too might be in a coffin.

The men assembled at Dallas to teach others to fly were a unique and interesting group.

There were the AV(N)'s, former cadets who had gone through Corpus Christi, Pensacola, or Jacksonville to win their wings and commission. Then they were the more colorful AV(T)'s who had been private pilots. Some had been crop dusters, others had owned small airports where they taught flying. A larger group consisted of week end pilots, business men who owned or flew rented planes and had enough time to earn commissions. Insurance salesman, oil men, singers, actors, farmers, lawyers, dancers, musicians—they were a varied and interesting lot.

Oil man Collins kept well drilling thriving even while he flew his three or four flights a day. Between hops he slipped into a hangar pay phone booth. In summer heat the phone booth clouded with steam as a sweating Collins directed his driller. When winter invaded the open hangar Collins shivered in the booth, then slipped into winter gear and hurried to his waiting Yellow Peril. Two insurance men, sensing opportunity, came to the rescue when the skipper announced two officers would be selected for duty Christmas Day. To be fair, the skipper said those two names would be drawn from the roster.

Two insurance men stepped in to put all pilots at ease. "We will issue a policy," they promised, "which will insure you *do not* have to serve Christmas Day. Buy this policy for ten dollars and, if your name is drawn, we will take the duty for you." In no time they amassed a tidy sum. A small group, mostly single AV(N)'s, refused to buy policies. When names were drawn, none of the policy holder names were drawn. The two insurance men also escaped, split their money, and were off to enjoy Christmas Day.

For new instructors, former cadets with perhaps 300 hours of flying time, climbing into the front cockpit of a Yellow Peril was a gut tightening experience. The student in that back cockpit was supposed to fly by "feel," with full control of the stick and rudders. Yet, at the near stalling speed of a landing approach, a sudden jerk of the stick or kick of a rudder could be fatal. This was especially true in "slips," a nose high left or right wing down maneuver that lost altitude in a hurry. Get too slow and the plane snapped over into a spin.

Faced with this dilemma, the more experienced instructor kept his right hand circled around the stick. Ready to tighten in a flash. The left hand circled the throttle and both feet inched close to but not touching the rudders. The less experienced instructors "rode" the controls. This was tough on students. They felt a heavy hand on the stick and rudders were stiff as the student pushed against an apprehensive foot. Most made it in spite of the handicap. Others who got "downs" were switched to veteran instructors.

"Ups" and "Downs" may have harked back to the days of the Romans. A "thumbs up" after a check ride meant the student was cleared for the next stage. A down turned thumb meant the ride was unsatisfactory. "B" stage, for example, included steep and gliding turns at altitude, "S" turns to land in a 50-foot circle, and spin entry and recovery. After the allotted hours of instruction, the student was up for a "check ride." This was with a veteran instructor, a "check pilot." He sat quietly in the front seat while the student taxied out, then as they climbed into the practice area, he quietly called for the various maneuvers. He could chop back the throttle at any time, waiting to see how the student handled the emergency.

Nose over quickly enough to prevent a stall and spin? Where was the wind? Which expanse below was safe for a dead stick landing? Make an error here and it was thumbs down for sure.

At the 50 foot circle the check pilot climbed out and sent the student off to "shoot circles." Usually four "Hits" were required. The student took off alone, circled left to 800 feet. With the circle off his left wing he throttled back to 65 knots, turned left and headed for the 50 foot circle with enough altitude to overshoot. To lose this extra altitude he made an "S" turn. Later in training, flying aircraft with flaps, he would lower flaps to lose that extra altitude and add power if he sank too low. But no extra throttle here. That was *verboten*. Land short or long and head around again.

Students at the next level, "C" stage, were required to use a side slip to hit circles. This maneuver required a more deft touch and skill. Check pilots had it easy. They could sit by the circle and watch. Instructors teaching slips to circles had it tougher. They had to show the maneuver to their student, then stay off the controls while he pulled the nose up near stalling speed, dropped a wing, and slid toward the circle. More experienced instructors first took students "upstairs" to practice slips where a sudden flop into a spin did not mean death.

Check pilots lounging near the circle often scurried as an incoming plane wavered. Some yelled "Throttle! Throttle!" as a plane started to land ten feet in the air. Often a student dropped in, smashing a wing or landing gear. One staggered from the shattered plane, waved to his stunned check pilot, and yelled, "Sir, that's four!"

The Yellow Perils were "tail draggers." This made teaching taxiing almost as difficult as teaching a student to solo. Sitting in the back cockpit, vision straight ahead was blocked by the hulking instructor in the front cockpit. Add to that the up tilted nose of the airplane and radial engine. The student leaned from side to side, guiding the plane with throttle and rudders.

Connerly, who had a student with only four hours of instruction and six hours from solo, urgently wanted a smoke. So, at an outlying field, he climbed out of the plane and told his student to practice taxiing on a bumpy stretch of grass. The area was clear of the circle where planes were landing and taking off in rapid succession. Connerly sat on his chute to puff at his weed and chat with check pilots. Behind him his student dutifully eased on throttle and rolled across the turf. A gentle wind gradually eased into gusts. The student shoved on more throttle to control direction. Now the plane began to bounce and, as the student added more throttle, lifted into the air.

Back at the circle the instructor jumped to his feet yelling. Too late now. His student was flying. Over the fence and climbing. As the frightened instructor watched the student, doing as he saw his instructor do in those scant four hours, added more throttle and circled for a landing. Then he throttled back and came gliding in.

As the student cut the throttle, the airplane staggered. "Go around, go around!" the instructor screamed. Perhaps the student heard. He slammed on full throttle. The Yellow Peril lurched and kept flying. Two more attempts and the plane dropped six feet to the turf. "Cut the throttle, chop the throttle!" the instructor yelled as he raced after the rolling airplane.

In spite of his goof, the instructor should have been proud. He taught so well his student soloed in *four* hours. That solo flight did not go in the student's folder. He got six more hours of instruction. Only check pilots at the circle knew what happened that gusty day and we didn't tell.

Seat belt checks were routine. When the instructor or check pilot arrived the student waited in the rear cockpit, engine ticking over. The check pilot or instructor returned the salute, then leaned over the rear cockpit to check the student's seat belt. There was no one to check the instructor's.

Chuck Farley walked out to give a "B" check ride. The student had soloed and received instruction in various simple maneuvers and S turns to circles. Capable of level flight maneuvers and not yet into aerobatics. Chuck returned the nervous salute, leaned over to check the student's seat belt, then climbed into the front cockpit. "Let's go," he ordered over the primitive gosport.

"And give me a good ride." He did not know it but one was in store.

The student taxied out to the big mat, waited his turn, and when the green light hit, shoved on full throttle. The Stearman picked up speed, forward pressure on the stick and the tail was up. Now they were climbing straight ahead. At two hundred feet, a critical spot, Chuck pulled back the throttle. Well trained, the student slammed the stick forward and down went the nose. Up went the check pilot. Chuck had forgotten to fasten his seat belt. He shot upward, flipped, and landed behind the rear cockpit. Chuck grabbed the cockpit rim and, fortunately, was straddling the fuselage. "Land it, land it!" he yelled. Under two hundred feet was not enough room to open the parachute.

With no safe landing place straight ahead, the student did what any properly instructed student should do. He shoved on power and began to climb. After all this was a check ride. At the proper altitude he circled left and started his approach to the field. With Chuck hanging on for dear life, he brought the plane in for a nice three point landing. So far he had an "up."

As the airplane rolled to a stop, Chuck tumbled off the fuselage. Still shaking, he climbed into the front cockpit and, in a voice that cracked midway, ordered, "Okay, let's try it again." Then he carefully fastened his seat belt. There were no more "cut guns" and the student got an "up."

Instructors and check pilots who imbibed too much in Big D the night before had one ally. This was the cool, often chilly air at four thousand feet. Even in the heat of August that cool air was up there, ready to cure a throbbing hangover. Slumped in the front cockpit, the still Bourbon breathed pilot came alive when the altimeter hit four thousand. The only instructor foiled was one whose student had not soloed and did not know how to reach four thousand.

Dougan, which was not his name, had a rep for enjoying the sauce. He was an excellent instructor and his students did well.

THE GUNS NOBODY HEARD
23 YEARS THAT CHANGED AMERICA FOREVER

He had an eight o'clock one morning. Not much time to slurp extra cups of hot coffee. Carrying his parachute, Dougan made it to the airplane and waved a limp salute. The quick and easy way to slip on a parachute was to hold it out front by the harness straps, swing it left and slip into the harness. Done properly, the straps went neatly over each shoulder as the 'chute slammed into your butt where it belonged.

Dougan swung and the momentum overwhelmed. He collapsed backward on the tarmac.

Dougan stood up, snapped 'chute harness into place, and climbed into the front cockpit. "Take 'er upstairs," he ordered. There cool air awaited, hangovers vanished in a flash, and the student had a great start on an "up."

Dougan had a day off and, when he came back to B.O.Q the bar was empty except for Fred, the friendly bar tender. "Gimme a Scotch and soda," Dougan ordered. "And where is everybody?"

"You just missed 'em," Fred grinned as he poured the drink. "A hurricane is coming in at Corpus. They expect high winds here so the Skipper ordered all our crates flown to Norman."

Dougan shrugged. "Well, sorry I missed it." He lifted his glass. "Let's drink to 'em."

Behind him, the base commander appeared in the doorway. "Lieutenant Dougan!" he exclaimed. "What are you doing here?"

Dougan slid off his stool and saluted. "Sir, I am standing by to fly the bar to a safe place."

Fred the bartender extended a glass. "Sir, your usual Scotch and water."

The captain took the glass, lifted it in a silent toast to his junior officer, and stifled a laugh. He too had once been a lieutenant.

Bye Bye B.O.Q.

Fortunately for some of us the roar of propellers and the smell of engine oil was replaced, when instruction rides permitted, by the pleasant aroma of perfume. We met some lovely ladies in Dallas.

A former college friend introduced a talented and strikingly beautiful young lady. In spare time, before she met her intended, she was a volunteer at the Air Raid Warning center in the Santa Fe building. (Those Japs could hit Dallas any time) Full time she worked as a model at Neiman Marcus. Her name was Peggy and yes, with the lanky Navy pilot properly recommended, she would go dancing. Anything was more fun than pushing those little airplanes around with a stick.

Each week Stanley Marcus, then in his mid thirties, emceed a style show in the Baker Hotel's Mural Room. A talented merchandiser and showman, Stanley attracted Dallas elite with the weekly gala. Time came to show off wedding gowns so why not bring in some live "grooms?" When Peggy asked for volunteers that was no problem. A Navy JG and a Marine Lieutenant, both in dress whites, stepped into the breach. No need to ask the Commandant for permission to participate in this venture with beautiful young ladies. We were at war!

After this "rehearsal" a real wedding followed. This meant leaving the B.O.Q where meals were served by white clad mess attendants, bed neatly made while you were flying, and the bar was just down the hall. There was no on base housing for married officers. In Dallas apartments were almost non-existent. Peggy found a woman who was chopping up the interior of an old two story house. This would become four apartments. Put your name on the list and wait. Finally the landlady called. Seventy-five dollars a month? We paid it gladly.

THE GUNS NOBODY HEARD
23 YEARS THAT CHANGED AMERICA FOREVER

The apartment was furnished. It was "in line." Enter the small living room, pass through the equally small dining room, through the tiny kitchen, and into the bedroom. No side doors. A huge vintage "ice box" lurked in the small kitchen. "I'll replace that with a refrigerator," the landlady promised. Like many landlady promises that would take time and come at any time. We felt we were stuck with the ancient ice box.

First couple for dinner bragged politely about the little apartment as they squeezed around the table in the snug dining room. Food on the table, wine poured, and the door bell rang. "We're here," a sweaty giant in coveralls announced, "gonna get rid of that old ice box and bring you a new fridge!"

Moment of decision. Send them away and who knew when they'd be back. So guests helped rush the food and dishes off the table. Then moved out chairs and pushed the table aside. Sweaty movers wheeled the ancient ice box through the living room and into the hall. Then they rolled in the refrigerator. They did not stay to help in the restoration.

Next dinner guests to enjoy the new refrigerator were the bride's parents. I knew this was a special evening. Parents of the bride still had to be convinced whether or not their daughter's catch should be thrown back. Unfortunately I had to hitch rides to and from the airfield. On this important evening my driver ride provider, who had no in laws waiting, paused to hit the BOQ bar before heading for Dallas. So I waited patiently with fellow riders and, waiting, had a couple. (Maybe it was three) The ride home was an hour late. At the apartment door I paused, then courage returning, pushed open the door and pitched in my cap. It skidded across the small living room floor and stopped at my father-in-law's feet. The in-laws sat quietly, inwardly wondering what their daughter had brought into the family. It would take them years to find out.

Peggy's father may not have been surprised. He had only to think back to the wedding. I had no car so Dad's was borrowed for the short honeymoon. He handed over the keys, then helped load a couple of suit cases in the trunk. Just to lighten the situation, and ignoring that the father of the bride did not laugh often, I asked, "Just what kind of dowry are you giving her?"

He put the suitcase in the trunk, then said evenly, "You must be out of your mind!"

Lesson one. Don't joke with a new father-in-law until you've had a few beers together or tangled with his fishing line a few times. Then again, maybe letting us use his one and only car and gasoline ration stamps for three days was dowry enough.

New cars were non-existent. A trusted dealer had an elderly Plymouth convertible priced at $650. (Like $6,500 today, or more) Pay the down and Pacific Finance would ante up the rest at four per cent. A payment book, with detachable monthly coupons, would ride with us across much of America. Tires looked okay and that was important. In tire stores, only retreads waited at steep prices.

Then orders came to fly 25 Yellow Perils to Terre Haute, Indiana. That was ominous. If Yellow Perils were being shipped out, pilots would be close behind. The gaggle of biplanes flew in loose formation. Senior leaders flew up ahead at 2,000 feet. Other aircraft followed spread wide so pilots could relax. Two or three bored pilots dropped below, hedge hopping over trees and farms. All went well until one, crossing the Red River, snagged a telephone line. The wire wrapped around the propeller. Like a fly on a string the plane buzzed back across the river in a sweeping arc and smacked down on the Texas side.

Another hedge hopper made it into Oklahoma, then hedge hopped across a wheat field. A wheel hit a post and bounced across an open area. With a wheel gone the pilot kept flying, circled, and landed in the clear area. It was a neat one wheel landing. Then he ran back to get the wheel, raced back to his downed plane, and dropped the wheel. *Voila!* A forced landing! It worked.

Back to Dallas orders were waiting. I was going to fly transports. First stop, Atlanta for instrument training. Peggy, although expecting, insisted she would go. The Plymouth made it and then the hunt for housing. Peggy found an upstairs room in a sprawling two story frame house. The owner cashed in big. The place was a bird house. From the upstairs bedroom the only way to get inside the house was go down a stairway, walk around the house, and enter the front door. We took it. This was war.

Then on to Roanoke, Virginia, and quarters in delightful Hotel Roanoke. What a break! Meals were served in the sumptuous main dining room. Our waiter flashed two diamonds, one in each front tooth. When he smiled you shared a view previously enjoyed by the crowned heads of Europe. Our instructors were Pennsylvania Central Airline captains. The aircrafts were sturdy twin engine Douglas DC-3's. They were tail draggers but sturdy and reliable. After flying open cockpit Yellow Perils, entering the side door of a DC-3 and walking to the cockpit was like entering the back door of a house and walking through to the front porch. The tarmac was somewhere far below and we would have to learn to find it with the wheels. Most of our time would be spent flying the radio range with a hood across our side of the windshield.

Alas, Roanoke was over too soon. The next station would be Olathe, Kansas, a long drive across West Virginia and Missouri where gasoline would be scarce and retreads waited. We entered West Virginia as night was falling. Up ahead, blast furnaces glowed. They were making iron for the far away war. For me it was getting closer.

A long line of cars waited patiently for the single gasoline pump up ahead. There was no way the supply of gasoline would hold out if we waited. A long walk to the harried pump man. He looked at the orders and nodded. "Come on up. You are next."

No one in the long line frowned or said a word as we drove past on our way to the pump. They knew there was a war and the Navy guy was headed for it.

More gasoline coupons and two tires later, St. Louis loomed ahead. Then a retread let go.

Orders had to be shown, papers signed, and an over priced retread was handed over. Put it on yourself, we are too busy selling retreads. Then across St. Louis and *bam!* Another retread popped. My exhausted Navy wife suddenly beamed. "Mother has a good friend here in St. Louis. I'll give her a call!" Do that. Maybe the good friend will invite us to dinner, or even let us stay over night in her cool guest bedroom.

"How nice to hear from you, Peggy," the good friend exclaimed. "Do call us again when you are in St. Louis!" Click!

Olathe is thirty miles or so South of Kansas City, Kansas. Here too housing was tight. A long waiting list for the little shacks on "Navy Hill." So it had to be Kansas City. Peggy zeroed in and found a small but comfortable house. She plunked down a hundred dollar deposit. If you follow with your arithmetic, the buying power was like one thousand bucks today. A steep deposit but a house. But this was war.

Three days later orders came through. Not for training in Olathe. Orders to head for San Francisco and who knew where after that. Now with San Francisco too far for the Plymouth and retreads, it seemed wise for Peggy to go back to Dallas and wait for our first born to arrive. She protested but it was a sad farewell.

Our landlord was no patriot. He kept our hundred dollar deposit. If I left Kansas to fight for freedom it sure as Hell would not be his.

Westward Ho!

Just two years earlier Pearl Harbor had been blasted by the Japanese Navy. Now Oahu seemed tranquil as our big seaplane landed in the bay and taxied to the beach. We were here to fly in the Naval Transport Service. Four engine Douglas R5D's waited at John Rogers Airport for us to take over and win the war. We would be co-pilots first, then go back to Olathe to fly DC'3. And then back to San Francisco to check out as plane commanders on the four engine jobs.

Weird, but this was war.

That first evening a former Dallas instructor now a command pilot asked, "Want to go with us? We are going to run a check on a plane just out of maintenance. Be a nice flight." Sure, why not. A chance to get an early ride in one of those big dudes.

It was a beautiful night. Lights glowed across Oahu. Above, stars twinkled in a deep purple sky. What must this have been like a scant two years earlier? The pilot locked the nose wheel, pushed the four throttles forward, and we raced down the long runway. Now we lifted off, the landing gear slammed home, and we climbed smoothly to five thousand feet. The pilot headed out over the ocean to clear air traffic, then circled lazily while the engineer ran his checks. With these completed, we headed for home.

Suddenly explosions flashed ahead, rising toward our level. Now the sky ahead was a canopy of explosions. "That's anti aircraft," our pilot yelled, slamming into a fast turn. He headed for Hilo. "Something must have panicked them. Let's go to Hilo and circle until they settle down." After a half hour of circling, we tried again. This time the night sky was quiet. Stars twinkled again. We landed without incident.

The Naval Air Transport Service was a fast moving life line to the far Pacific. While ships carried troops, weapons, and supplies NATS, as it was abbreviated, ferried key personnel, top priority cargo, and mail.

Cargo might be top secret or classified. On a flight to Guam, armed sailors guarded canvas draped cases lined up each side of the companionway. Mouse like squeaks came from the crates.

"What's in the crates?"

"Sorry, Sir," the armed guard replied. "The crates are top secret."

Okay, we flew the crates to Guam. Later, after the war, the secret came out. Doc Adams, a rotund and genial gray topped inventor, said, "During the war I pitched an idea to President Roosevelt. He bought it. We planned to put little incendiary bombs on bats. Then drop them over Tokyo. They'd fly down, crawl in those paper houses, and burn 'em down. (The bats did not make it to Japan. The A bomb beat them to it.)

JOE JAMES

"What's in the crates?"

Quarters on Oahu were nice. Two officers to a room. Comfortable single beds and a steward who came in each day, made the bed, and cleaned the room. The officers' mess was a short walk and a "snack shack" even closer.

There was little time for us new arrivals to enjoy the B.O.Q. My first flight west would be to Kwajalein. This formerly luxuriant tropical island, once covered by groves of palm and coconut trees, was now a long stretch of sand. A few battered coconut stumps and shattered concrete pill boxes edged above the sand. A short time earlier men had died on this desolate stretch of sand. Now rows of small tents flanked a long walk. Behind each tent a small wind mill spun in the breeze, pushing a short stick up and down in small tub. "Those are washing machines," a sailor explained. "Don't know how well they wash, but it helps break the boredom."

Time to find quarters for the night. Ask at the quonset. The chief behind the counter had a sleep assignment for us. "Just go to the second quonset. Pick any bed."

The place was dark. Great, we'd have our pick of beds. Snap on the light and hold on, Nelly. These cots had no mattress. No sheets either. And the pillow had no cover. There had to be some mistake. Back to the office frustrated as only a lieutenant senior grade can be frustrated.

"Chief, those cots don't have mattresses. No sheets, and no pillow slips!"

"Yes, Sir, I know," the chief smiled. "Welcome to Kwajalein!"

The Far Pacific

Kwajalein was the last stop before NATS flew to Manus, to Guam and soon on to Okinawa. From Oahu to Kwajalein a convenient midway point was Johnson Island. This sliver of sand had a runway that stretched from water's edge to water's edge. A seaplane landing area, well lighted at night, paralleled the land plane runway. Many a plane commander invited his new co-pilot to make a night landing, then laughed and said, "You'd better move over. You're about to land in the water."

Leave Kwajalein in any direction and a vast expanse of Pacific awaited. Our destination was Manus, an island in the Admiralties not far from Australia and Japanese occupied New Guinea. As we neared the equator the equatorial front lurked. Towering thunderheads stretched across the horizon and upward to 60,000 feet. Without oxygen we did not fly above ten thousand feet. There was no dodging this line of thunderstorms. Watch lightning flash then pick a place where it didn't. There was no turning back.

Finally the welcome sight of Manus. Japs were still on Rabaul and within striking distance. As we approached two Marine Corsairs raced out to meet us, then flew alongside until we settled toward the long runway. The shell runway stretched the length of the island. Unlike battle ravaged Kwajalein palm trees stood tall and green. On the far side of the island natives lived in grass huts, exactly as before Marines hit the beach.

As dawn was breaking, a brisk walk to the runway seemed a good idea. Much of the island was still asleep. In the distance an aircraft engine sputtered, then became a steady roar. A strange and blurred object moved into position. Now it sped closer, lifting into the air. This was a ghost, a wraith from World War I. No, it was a lumbering amphibian, two wings, and a pusher prop spinning not far from the pilot's head. A gunner stood in the nose gripping a mounted machine gun. This was a British Walrus, relic from World War I, heading out to protect Manus. A generation separated it from the Corsairs that escorted us in.

On a later flight from Kwajalein to Guam no towering line of thunderstorms barred our way. Only a vast stretch of calm Pacific. At night water and sky joined in total blackness. Then, far off on the horizon, a light glowed. The co-pilot, sitting alone in the cockpit while others slept, called for the navigator. He climbed into the vacant seat, stared into the darkness, and shook his head. "That's Venus. You won't see a light out here. Never." He pointed at the right wing tip. "Truk is over there. About a hundred and fifty miles."

The Japs on Truk had been by-passed. "They don't have radar," the navigator reasoned. "To catch us, they would have to get awfully lucky or," he grinned impishly, "I would have made a very bad mistake." He turned on the radio. A woman was talking, in English. "Today a Japanese officer on Tarawa killed thirty Marines," she bragged. "The Americans are being driven back into the sea."

"That's Tokyo Rose," the navigator muttered.

An eerie feeling, knowing the Japs were out there in the darkness, a hundred and fifty miles away. Our four engines droned faithfully, carrying us rapidly away from Truk and Tokyo Rose.

Guam emerged at dawn. White cliffs rose from the sea. During the invasion, frightened Japanese families jumped from those cliffs. Battered landing craft still lay in the surf. Above, on the plateau, Agana airport ran as smoothly as Love Field back in Dallas. "Take a break," the routing officer suggested. "You're not scheduled to head back until late tomorrow."

"Well look who's here," a Marine major called. He was Tom W. a former flight instructor at Grand Prairie. "We've got an extra bunk at our tent," he welcomed. "Come on and bunk with us." Tom's tent was a jeep ride from the airport. The jungle rose close behind it. "There's still some Japs in there," Tom said. "They slip up here at night to steal food." The next morning he had an idea. "I've got to go fly combat air patrol. Why don't you come with us? I'll give you a cockpit check. That Corsair is a cinch to fly. Handles like Yellow Peril, only a Hell of a lot faster. It'll be a piece of cake."

That would be fun but no thanks. From four engines to one engine could get dicey. One goof and we would both get a court martial. "Okay," the major nodded, and handed over a forty five automatic. "Keep this handy, just in case a Jap slips in."

Our plane was loaded and ready late the next afternoon. We left Guam and headed for Hawaii. Our first stop would be Kwajalein, then Johnson Island, and finally Hawaii. It was July 31, 1945, a date we would long remember. The navigator set the course. "The Japs sank a cruiser last night," he announced.

"The *Indianapolis*. No time to get a fix after the torpedoes hit. Just a May Day. Any survivors are out there in the water. We may fly right over them."

Soon it was night. But now there was a moon. It cast soft, undulating shadows on water six thousand feet below. Somewhere down there men were struggling to stay alive. As the engines droned, and with the autopilot in control, we watched the endless stretch of water.

Nothing. It was a sad and terrible feeling. One that would linger the rest of our lives.

Survivors were not found until August 2nd, two days later. By then many had been killed by ravaging sharks. Just a flicker of light and we, or some other passing plane, might have saved them.

Back to Olathe

After four months it was time to leave the Pacific and go back to Olathe, another "island" in Kansas far from the stress of war. It would be a brief respite, then we'd go back to San Francisco to check out as plane commanders on the flights

The Navy R4-D (Douglas DC-3) that carried us east from San Francisco was combination passenger-cargo. Crates lined the center aisle; rows of bench seats snapped down on each side of the fuselage. Rough air bounced the plane and some pilot-passengers, not used to bouncing in the rear, began to turn green. That is when the co-pilot came back and announced, "You guys are lucky. I'd sure like to be going back to Corpus Christi. I'd get me a batch of fresh shrimp, pick out one, and bite off the head!" That did it. The "green ones" grabbed barf bags.

First a stop in Dallas to see bride and tiny daughter Michael, then on to Olathe. The war time terminal at Dallas' Love Field was the size of a current McDonalds. A metal fence separated non-passengers from the tarmac. Our plane rolled up to the fence and a stairway was wheeled out. There was Peggy, waiting for a husband she had not seen in six months. Then back to her parents' home for a first look at our baby. It was a wonderful, but brief, homecoming.

Peggy found a house on Olathe's "Navy Hill." It was small, but it was a house. No garage, small furnace room, tiny kitchen, dining room, bedroom, and bath. We were glad to get it. Then Peggy went back to Dallas to fetch our daughter.

Now it was back to flying. Olathe was the hub for two routes. One went east to Washington, D.C., New York, and Chicago. The other headed west to Winslow and Phoenix, Arizona. There it connected with flights coming from the West Coast. The choice, if we were lucky, was easy. Take the Winslow, Phoenix run. Better weather. Only one drawback. Now and then the return flight detoured to Fort Worth. Passengers would be battle fatigue casualties, sedated men in three-high bunks. Walking past them to reach the cockpit was always an ordeal, a grim reminder that they must have been through Hell. In Fort Worth they went to a military hospital and hopefully recovery.

Varner, a fellow pilot, wanted to sell plays he had written. Letters to New York had been of no avail so Varner asked for the New York run. He would go after producers in their dens. It was a bad decision. Weather could get terrible. The climax came approaching Chicago. The weather was foul. Varner got lost. Forget radio beams. He finally broke out along the lake front and followed it to the airport. Thoroughly whipped down and still shaking, Varner announced, "They can come and get this airplane. And they can come and get me. I am not flying any more." And he did not. Who knows what Broadway lost.

Flying in bad weather, as Varner learned, could be nerve

wracking. Today's airline pilots punch in coordinates on computers and the airplane flies to the destination. Flying in bad weather during World War II a pilot had only a radio range to guide the way to an airport. Each radio station on a route sent out a sound pattern like a cross. This created four beams of solid sound, a steady drone or hum. That left four sectors between the beams. In one a "dit dah" steadily repeated. In the adjoining sector, a "dah dit" clicked.

Flying in driving rain or amid the crackle of lightning, a pilot got on the beam and headed for the station. Drift right off the beam and "dah dit" suddenly emerged from the steady hum. Drift farther and grew louder. Drift left and "dit dah" sounded.

The hum of the beam grew louder as the station neared. The pilot, with flaps and gear down, waited for the "cone of silence." The hum grew louder and louder and then, over the station, complete silence. That was the signal to chop power and drop to the minimum approach altitude. If the pilot could see the runway, quickly chop more power and land. If only driving rain or fog, climb out fast. The pilot might try a second approach or go to an alternate airport.

Kansas City's airport was one of the worst places for an instrument approach. The airport was in a hollow, with tall buildings just beyond. Find the station, drop to the 400 foot minimum, and if only driving rain it was full power and climb out fast in a climbing turn to miss those buildings. During the war at least one airplane didn't turn. Today the airport is far from town and pilots no longer sweat in cold cockpits as they ride the beam.

Social life was slow. Before Varner's Chicago demise, he and Marline invited us to dinner. Their little Navy Hill house was aglow with candles. Varner wore dress whites and Marline was lovely in a stunning cocktail dress. We might have been dining on the Riviera. Varner filled wine glasses. We made toasts to peace and a normal life. Then our hosts walked to the door, opened it and threw glasses into the darkness. We hesitated, then followed and threw ours. "We would throw them in the fireplace," Varner apologized, "but we don't have a fireplace."

That sudden impulsive act may have been a revolt against the war and events that had us locked in on "Navy Hill."

No More 'Smoke on the Water'

Suddenly peace exploded. Not one word had been leaked about an atomic bomb. What was it? Sounded terrible, horrifying. But it stopped the war and saved thousand of Americans destined to die on Japan's beaches. Terrible, yes, but to all in the vast Pacific or headed that way it was a wonderful bomb indeed.

Events moved quickly. Arming for war is a slow and drawn out process. Men are drafted, trained, and finally moved into combat. When war ends, warriors can be back in civilian clothes in a month. As World War II ended, points were issued based on length of service. If you were in the States and had enough points, a commanding officer had to issue release orders quickly. At Olathe the squadron commander pleaded. "Stay on and I'll get you a promotion. I need pilots to keep this airline running." But for many, the appeal of civilian life was too great.

Some NATS pilots went to the airlines. The pay was good but it meant back into the hassle. Listening to the dit dahs and dah dits while bouncing along the airways. There had to be a better way. Money was not everything.

An aviation magazine, Southern Flight, had a job. Fly the rush of new private airplanes and report. According to the Civil Aeronautics Association, the sky would soon be full of private fliers. They could be right. A new plane debuted almost every month. The Globe Swift, Johnson Rocket, Culver Cadet, North American Navion, Beech Bonanza, Republic Seabee, Bellanca.

North American's Navion was among the first. Our publisher sensed a scoop. "Trappo is going to Los Angeles to pick up his demo," he announced. "It will be the first Navion in Texas.

"Go with Trappo and fly back with him in his Navion." Trappo was the nick name for Jimmy Marshall, an enthusiastic airplane salesman who had flown since barnstorming days. Off we went on American Airlines. Trappo sat next to Walter Pigeon, a leading movie star who had been in Dallas boosting a film. (This was a switch. Flying with a pigeon.)

In Los Angeles Pigeon offered a ride to the hotel in his limo. As he dropped us off at our hotel, a trim and beautiful lady rushed over and beamed, "Hello, Walter darling!" He kissed each cheek, then she was off. "Who was that?" Trappo asked.

Pigeon shrugged. "I don't know. Never saw her before."

The Navion was a low wing all metal airplane. Retail price was $7,500. Trappo was in a hurry to get his "demonstrator" back to Texas. When the plane was finally rolled out on North American's tarmac dusk was approaching.

Trappo climbed into the night, then headed east above a long line of cars lighting the highway far below. "What would you do" I asked nervously, "if the engine quits?"

"I'd get down there with them ground boxes," Trappo

countered. Ground boxes, in his lingo, were cars.

After a Phoenix stop and a few hours sleep, we were up at dawn and flying east. When Odessa, Texas, approached Trappo confided, "I've got me a bird dog in Odessa. He'll have some hot prospects at the airport."

Trappo made a sweeping dive at the field, then flew low and fast so all could see the Navion. Then he pulled up in a steep climbing turn, popped the landing gear down, and settled gracefully on the long runway. His "bird dog" and prospects were eagerly waiting.

Back in Dallas Peggy found a little house for $8,000. The bank loan was four per cent. Total tax, interest and principal $45 a month. We could live on that. Prices were still low but friends warned an upsurge was coming. "Don't buy a low cost house," they urged. "Go into debt. We're gonna have inflation. Always do after a war."

They were right. But $8,000 seemed steep at my starting salary. We did splurge and, in the heat of summer, had asbestos pumped into the attic. We never dreamed asbestos would be the demon it became.

Attic insulation helped but summer heat was oppressive. The next door neighbor bought one of the new window "air conditioners." He invited us over to "get cool." We stayed a few minutes and left. No use getting accustomed to that cool air when we would have to go back later to our hot house.

Television was just making its debut. Black and white sets with small screens. First models, out of reach for many of us, were displayed in store windows. At night, when stores were closed, small crowds gathered on the sidewalk to watch this amazing new invention. Later, when prices came down, new owners gazed at wrestling and cooking shows. News programs were primitive. No crews with cameras rushed to the scene of an accident. There was no way to record away from the station. The recorder in the station was a "wire recorder," a big reel of wire, cumbersome. There was a lot of "fill time" between programs. Singers and musicians were hired to come in and fill the gaps. Cooking shows got top billing. Night time material got better as "Uncle Miltie" Berle took the lead. Everything was "live" and attempts at drama put a great demand on actors who had to know their lines but also timing.

Wrestling was far different from today's TV. Violence was limited to body slams and throwing an opponent out of the ring. Referees helped involve the audience. If a wrestler was gouging an eye, the referee pretended not to see it. "Look what he's doing," fans would scream.

Almost every wrestler had a "Killer" hold or maneuver which, if he got to use it, immobilized his opponent like the strike of a cobra or the squeeze of a python. A Fort Worth wrestler gripped an opponent's head between his ankles and flopped him around the ring like a mackerel. There was no escape.

It was an awkward time for TV, just learning to walk. But audiences did not complain. They were perfectly happy with this amazing new piece of furniture that glowed brightly, even if the wrestlers were faking it.

'Freelancing' with a Short Lance

When a "depression" hit the flying business all the private planes predicted for backyards did not arrive. It was time to bail out.

Since pulp magazines had already bought some of my flying stories, becoming a "freelancer" seemed a logical step. The term had real meaning. In the days of knighthood a wandering knight looking for a sponsor was called a "free lancer." Unlike later aspirants who too often worked for "free" the earlier lancer had someone who bought oats for his horse, put meat on the table for Sir Knight, and squirted oil on his squeaky coat of mail. With a typewriter it would be different.

"Pulp magazines still filled the racks at the drug stores. Printed on cheap "pulp" paper with colorful dramatic covers, subjects for a "freelancer" were many. There were Westerns, Detective, Aviation, Horror, and Love and Romance. My best prospect was *Wings*, a Fawcett pulp where air battles had long featured the Camels, Spads, and Fokkers of World War I. Now it was ready for stories about the flying Aces of WW II.

For a new author, *Wings* paid a penny a word if it bought a story. A typical monthly salary for a returning vet with a degree was $350. To match it the "freelancer" had to sell 35,000 words. The first attempt, a 9,000 word short story, earned a $90 check.

The next attempt was a thirty thousand word "novelette." Today's word processor or computer would have made free lancing easy. In those days the final draft was typed with a carbon back up. Make a typo and often the entire page had to be retyped.

The novelette sold. The next one bounced. Editor Reiss tucked in a note. "Your protagonist needs more development."

What was a "protagonist"? If one was in my novelette I had better find him or her and get busy. If the editor had said "hero" it sure would have helped.

More typewriter banging and one month the editor bought two novelettes. "We'll use your name on one," the editor said, "but we can't use it on two in the same issue. Your other story will be by 'John Starr.'" No problem as long as he got the correct name on the check.

An inquisitive neighbor asked, "What do you do at home all day?" Told I was writing fiction he asked, "Do you just sit there with a bottle of bourbon and write." He didn't know much about freelancing. That might work for a single "freelancer" but one with a family would have to sip lemonade—if lemons were cheap.

Pulp magazines did well until television sets were flickering blue lights in almost every home. Then pulp magazines dwindled on drug store racks. My editor became a literary agent. Some freelancers rode it out and moved on to books.

THE GUNS NOBODY HEARD
23 YEARS THAT CHANGED AMERICA FOREVER

Today the pulp story techniques are still there. A forty or fifty thousand word book, once a freelancer's delight at $400 or $500, now earns far more. Some even become movies.

Now I know I put away my lance too soon.

Of Cars and People

The Studebaker dealer needed an ad man and part time salesman. Right off I offered an idea later to be picked up by golfers and race car drivers. "Let's pay some of those wrestlers to wear our Studebaker logo on their shirt backs."

"No," the boss said firmly. "Those wrestlers spend a lot of time on their backs. And besides, ours might not win."

The 1947 Studebaker was a fresh design. A dramatic change from the long hoods and small rear windows of other cars. The car was stick shift. Studebaker had sold the hydromatic shift to Oldsmobile. We had to sell against that. And there was much to learn about selling, and people.

A prim and proper prospect walked in and announced, "I want a price on a Champion. Don't try to sell me anything else. My Champion is out there. Get it appraised and tell me what you can do."

Fortunately he was up against a veteran salesman. He

waited with his prospect while the appraiser sized up the trade in. A red Land Cruiser turned slowly on the show room turn table. "I could never drive one of those," the little man announced firmly.

"And why not?"

"Because I drive some nice ladies to church every Sunday. If I drove up in that big showy car they would really give it to me for putting on airs."

"Now hold on a minute," the salesman suggested. "The Bible says something like 'Be a good Christian and you shall be rewarded, pressed down and overflowing.'"

The prospect grinned. "Get me a quote on that Land Cruiser."

He liked the quote. On the next Sunday, the ladies were in for a surprise. And the little man, pressed down and overflowing, was ready for them.

Another prospect came in demanding a Land Cruiser. The new model spinning on the turn table was the latest by designer Raymond Loewy. It had an eye-catching chrome point on its nose.

(This prompted some owners to add a small propeller.) The prospect wanted that bright green Land Cruiser with the needle nose and he had cash.

The next day the needle nose owner robbed a Dallas bank. He raced East on Highway 80 in the only green Land Cruiser with a needle nose in that part of Texas. Lawmen waited for him and a shot across his bow put a hole in a bright green door. The short time owner headed for the penitentiary. He also bore the label "stupid."

Now There Was a Mayor

The Dallas of 1949 was just four years past the war and change was slow. Later mayors would become "citified," wear blue suits, shoes with tassels, and never say a cuss word. Maybe Dallas' post war mayor was the last of his kind, like the fast disappearing horned toad. He was tall, lean and rugged, wore cowboy boots and a Stetson pushed back over a strong and weathered face. He came to Dallas as a young man from east Texas, worked hard, and was now the president of the Mercantile Bank and mayor of Dallas. His name was R.L. Thornton and he was a Texan to remember.

When a "big shot" came to town that often called for an official welcome. The word "celebrity" had not yet been coined and a "big shot" really had to be one. One of them was Baron Silvercruy who came to open the Belgian exhibit at the State Fair of Texas. The Baron was camped at the Baker Hotel, Main and Akard, in the heart of downtown Dallas. The boss sent a new Studebaker convertible to pick up the mayor and take him and the Baron to the ribbon cutting.

A line of cars waited at the Baker. We joined them. "Where's the Baron?" Mayor Thornton asked.

"The Baron is taking a nap," a Belgian aide answered. "He always takes a nap at noon."

"Damn!" the Mayor muttered. "Wish I had time to take me a nap." He kicked a tire, then grinned and settled in his seat to wait for the snoozing Baron.

The State Fair of Texas, a big deal in Big D every October, always counted on the mayor for the Grand Opening. But this time a call for the mayor came with the fair well under way. "Got a call from a couple," Thornton explained as we drove to the fair. "They asked me to come for a mortgage burning. Let's avoid the main gate. Too dang many people."

We pulled up at a locked side gate. An attendant, relaxed on a camp stool, waved us away. "You all can't come in this gate," he ordered, still comfortably seated. "Go to the Main Gate."

Thornton, who in his battered Stetson looked like a visiting rancher, beckoned to the gate guard. "Young man," he called, "come here a minute."

The gate guard shrugged and got up from his stool. "Yes sir, but like I said this gate is for deliveries only. You all got to go to the Main Gate."

Thornton beckoned for him to come closer and said, "Young man, I'm R.L. Thornton, chairman of this State Fair. Now open the damn gate!"

The gate was open in seconds and we drove in to find the "mortgage burners." An elderly couple waited beside an upright 55 gallon metal drum. The mayor shook hands and said, "Howdy! I'm R.L. Thornton. Now let's get going." The couple jointly held their paid off mortgage over the empty drum. The mayor struck a match on his boot, then lit the paper.

"Who were they?" I asked as we drove back to the gate.

"Just some nice folks who called in," Thornton answered. "Never saw 'em before. But it is not every day somebody gets to burn a mortgage. That's when it's nice to be the mayor."

On my next trip to Dallas, I'll call and ask if the mayor is available to burn a mortgage. Just to see if times have changed.

Play It Purty!

As the war faded, the economy stirred and prices began a slow rise. There was another change in the wind. It was the beat of "country western" music.

Over in Louisiana a young upstart with a sexy voice, catchy undulating beat, and swivel hips moved on the scene. Slowly at first. He drove alone to appear in the Big D Jamboree, stopping on the way at Shoemaker's rambling nursery on the outskirts of Mineola. "Elvis would stop by here for a Big Red and a Moon Pie," owner Shoemaker said. "Then he'd be off to Dallas."

In Dallas the late Johnny Hicks rallied talent for his Saturday night "Big D Jamboree."

He booked young yet undiscovered Elvis for $150. And he signed another up and coming singer, John Cash, for $175. That included a side man.

Johnny, who was about five foot six, had his own band. It was "Big Shorty and the Pile Drivers." When the then towering Shamrock hotel opened in Houston, Johnny's band was booked to play. It was not the spotlight band. That was a big band with a young singer named Merve Griffin. Johnny's country music band played when the big band took a break. The lively beat of country music scored with the dancers.

During a break, singer Griffin came over to ask a favor. "Would you mind," he asked Johnny, "if I sing with your band?"

"Sure," Johnny agreed. "What shall we play?"

Griffin hopped on the bandstand. "San Antonio Rose!"

Riding with the surge in country music, Johnny booked shows across the south. He arrived at Hot Springs early to check on his cast. Moving around the hotel lobby and pool, he accounted for all except a new singer, Hank Williams.

THE GUNS NOBODY HEARD
23 YEARS THAT CHANGED AMERICA FOREVER

"I got his room number," Johnny recalled, "and went up there. Knocked on the door and Hank hollered to come in. He was sitting up in bed. Had on his cowboy hat, no clothes, and his cowboy boots. Had his guitar across his lap and a bottle of Jack Daniel sitting on his guitar case.

Hank said, 'Johnny, I've just written a song. See what you think.'"

Then Williams, propped against the headboard and with cowboy hat pushed bank, began to sing:

"Hear the lonesome whippoorwill

It sounds too blue to fly..."

When he finished Hank asked, "Johnny, what do you think?"

"I didn't hesitate," Hicks recalled. "I said Hank you've got a winner."

I'm So Lonesome I Could Cry is still a favorite today.

Show and Sell

Enough with the needle nosed cars, it was time to head for Fort Worth and a new advertising and selling experience.

The company was then known as Panther Oil and Grease. No panthers but lots of oil, grease and roof coating to be sold. And it was being sold by direct salesman across the breadth of the nation. The president was a bright man who knew how to motivate salesmen and stressed demonstrating products and use of visual aids. His copyrighted technique was "Selling Through The Eyes." A "Book of Evidence," filled with testimonials from satisfied customers, was used to back up the salesman's claim. Small samples of roof coating were bent and twisted to show how the product withstood heat and cold

New salesmen were attracted by ads. "Earn Ten Thousand Dollars A Year" was the invitation. Earning ten thousand, in 1951, a salesman could live high on the hog. Belong to a country club, own a Cadillac. This was true. And a good salesman could do very well indeed. One gentleman up in Utah earned thirty thousand a year. He had a calm relaxed mien, blue eyes that inspired confidence, and was an honest sincere man who believed in the products he sold. Never a complaint from his customers.

All salesmen hired long distance were not as accomplished or trusting. One on the East Coast came on like gang busters. Orders flowed in. With a start like that he would be right up there with the man from Utah. There was even an order sold to Arthur Godfrey, the popular television personality and ukelele strummer.

Orders were checked before shipment. All orders from this new hot shot were pipe dreams. None were legitimate. And none were shipped.

Good companies are always alert to new potential. Detergents were coming along fast.

A new and inviting field. Panther created a new product, for restaurant and hotel mechanical dishwashers. "Before you create sales literature," the boss suggested, "you need to go out in the field and demonstrate the product. Test it with customers, get their comments. Then come back and create sales literature and ways to demonstrate. I'll send a veteran salesman with you. Watch him and learn."

Wiley was a crack salesman. Homespun, unpretentious he inspired immediate trust.

Wiley was not too sure about this new product but he was going to give it his best. He also had a great sense of humor.

After a long day pitching our product in Oklahoma, we checked into a rambling frame hotel. (True motels had not yet arrived.) A porter stepped eagerly forward to carry our bags to the second floor room. The porter led us into our room, placed our bags on a low stand, and turned to get his tip. "Quick!"

Wiley suddenly exclaimed, "lock that door."

The porter rushed to the door, then stopped short. "You mean lock it inside?"

"Yes, yes!" Wiley urged. "I am about to have one of my fits!"

The porter was gone in a flash.

Sometimes the joke was on us. As we approached a drug store, Wiley suggested, "Why don't you make this pitch?"

Okay, after watching Wiley it was time to give it a whirl. "Boss is in the back," the soda jerk advised. "Just head on back. He knows you are coming."

A short wait, then the owner emerged. grinning pleasantly. Instead of hair, his head was covered with sculpted hair of black rubber.

Words failed, the name of the dish washing compound was forgotten.

"What you selling," the rubber topped man grinned.

I didn't know. I turned and scurried for the door. Behind me a I made one drug store owner's day.

"Hair Raising" Drama

Life in the early fifties was bustling. The ten thousand a year dream was out there for us all but my four hundred a month left much to go. The salary was not enough to buy one of the new power mowers. So the vacant lot, filled with grass burrs, had to be groomed with a hand pushed job. We did manage a black and white Emerson television set. That opened a vast realm of viewing. There was wrestling and cooking. Taping was done on crude wire wheels so any stage show had to be live from beginning to end. As a result there was little drama. But then came a delightful newspaper announcement. *Hair Raising Tales*, was scheduled.

This catchy title got our attention well in advance. After nothing but wrestling and cooking shows we were ready for some action. The title flashed and we settled back to what would be the first drama on television. A dynamic young man opened the show. Sitting at his desk, he talked for ten minutes, holding our rapt attention. We watched closely, waiting for some foul and evil killer to knock him off and get the mystery rolling. Then we realized we were the "victims." He was selling a fantastic new hair shampoo.

The occasional drama that did come along got a big build up and audience. One of these was backed with the mournful lyrics of "Cold, Cold Heart." It did much for Hank Williams but not much for drama. And that was understandable. All action had to be live. Actors of that era may have been the greatest ever. There were no retakes. Amazingly few lines were muffed.

Housing was still reasonable, if you had money. Our thirty-year-old, two story house with a non working coal furnace was ours for twelve thousand dollars. Anything higher than that had to be a mansion. Then a house began to take shape a few blocks away. Two stories, fresh design. Rumor was this house would cost fifty thousand dollars. We gasped at the thought and sneaked over to check it out. The owner drove up as we poked through the frame work. "Great house," we told him, "did you design it?"

"Oh no," he answered, "I hired me a arch i teck." (No, that is not misspelled.)

Our own experienced house needed remodeling. Remove one wall section of the hall and the small kitchen would suddenly be larger. Peggy invited a talented home improver neighbor to come over and show how to do the job. He stood in the hallway, surveyed the plaster covered wall, and said, "Is this the wall you want to take out?"

Peggy said, "Oh yes, this is it."

Our friend Oscar picked up a sledge hammer, hefted it lightly, and slammed it into the wall. Then he said, "That is how you get started."

Ten Not So Grand

Suddenly great news came from Dallas. A baking organization needed an ad man. The salary would be that dreamed of ten thousand. I applied and got the job.

Jack Gordon, witty Fort Worth Press columnist, termed it neatly: "He slid out of the grease and into the dough." The job was with Mrs Baird's, a family owned baking organization. The dreamed of ten grand was there but so was a surprise. "We only pay once a month," my new boss explained. "I hope that doesn't squeeze you but that is the way we pay our executives."

It was nice to be an "executive" even if it was tough to wait a month. When the check finally arrived, the dreamed of $833 a month was clipped by Social Security and withholding. Worse still, in less than three years the touted buying power of ten thousand dollars had waned. No Cadillac or European vacation. Instead it was still an ongoing effort to cover the bills. Surely, back in Fort Worth, my replacement by now had increased the dream salary to twenty grand.

Texas gets hot in the summer. Company cars were provided for us "executives" but, in the stifling heat we rolled down the windows and sweated. Suddenly the boss was driving cool. The secret was a new and startling invention: an air conditioner. Installed in the trunk, it took up a lot of space but somehow this new gadget produced cool air. Our boss enjoyed it, then okayed the trunk cooler for company cars. It was a new and delightful experience, driving in sweltering heat with windows rolled up. Yes, *rolled* up. Powered windows were still somewhere on a drawing board.

Another new auto item was a seat belt. This was a single strap across the lap. These had to be added like trunk air conditioners. Auto manufacturers were not sure the public wanted these devices. It was one thing to have them on airplanes but in cars? An intrusion on comfort. Shoulder restraints were in the far distant future.

Opening a wrapper and taking out slices of bread is as close as most people get to the bakery business. But go through the doors and a powerful tantalizing aroma envelopes you. Fresh bread baking. Then into a vast room of huge thumping mixers, long troughs (bakers pronounce it "troe") of rising dough, lines of moving conveyors, and piping hot fresh baked loaves tumbling from ovens. A far cry from Mrs. Baird's wood fired oven that baked forty loaves at a time and launched this family business in Fort Worth.

The story was unique. Truly one that could happen only in a burgeoning America. In 1908 Mrs. Ninnie Baird was baking bread for her family. When Mrs. Baird baked, she often baked more than needed and gave extra loaves to neighbors. They loved it and even then called it "Mrs Baird's Bread." When her husband became ill, Mrs. Baird had to support her family. She went into the baking business. At first her sons carried hot bread in baskets and delivered it to homes in the neighborhood. Then a sales wagon was purchased and Ned, a patient horse, pulled the wagon. Finally the sons bought a car, cut off the top behind the front seat, and added a box body.

That was history. Now there were bakeries in Fort Worth, Dallas, Abilene, and Houston. The small Dallas bakery was about to be replaced with a huge new plant on just completed North Central Expressway. Roland, one of Mrs. Baird's four sons, was the Baird in charge of the Dallas plant. He was a private pilot and, as the new plant neared completion, he had sign painters put a huge "Mrs Baird's" on the roof. Now an aerial photo was needed. PR man Jim Fuller at fast growing Bell Aircraft helped. He sent one of those new whirly birds over to take an aerial shot. Paul Crume, Dallas Morning News Columnist, saw unique possibilities. "What," he asked, "if Bell Helicopter next wants to borrow yeast to help their helicopters rise?"

Mrs. Ninnie Baird, while not active in day to day operations, was Chairman of The Board and meetings were held in her Fort Worth home. The opportunity to meet her came unexpectedly. *Business Week* magazine sent a writer to do a story on this unusual family business. Roland Baird gave the writer a "special treat," a ride from Dallas across thirty miles of sky in his four place single engine Cessna 190, a vivid contrast to the families first horse and wagon.

Mrs. Baird's home was a neat cottage. Not large but warm and inviting. She patiently answered questions. Then, when the writer had finished and launched into chit chat, she moved quietly into the kitchen and went to work. While the flow of conversation continued in the small living room, Mrs. Baird's was busy in her kitchen. A nudge aroused the photographer. His picture of Mrs Baird at her kitchen oven proved to be a classic. Moments later she brought in a large plate of warm and welcome cookies. When we left, she handed me a paper bag filled with cookies. "For your youngsters," she said. They were destined to enjoy cookies that really were "Mrs Baird's."

With the new plant nearing completion and tours coming up, we often worked late. One summer night I left for home as dusk descended. Pulling out of the lot, I crossed Central Expressway and turned north on the service road. Something new had just gone up alongside the service road.

It was a baseball batting cage. A high wire mesh fence surrounded the operation with a ball throwing machine on the pitcher's mound. There was no batter swinging at the moment. Just a lone young man sitting on a folding chair by the gate. Pay your money, pick up a bat, and swing away at base balls as they whizzed across the plate. The young man ball seller was also owner. This was his first venture into the sports business. He was Lamar Hunt. Later he founded the Dallas Texans football team, could not get an NFL franchise, started the American Football Conference, and now owns the Kansas City Chiefs. The AFC's annual championship trophy is named for Lamar. He also named the Super Bowl. Lamar has never owned a baseball team. Probably because he knows no pitcher as consistent as the one he had in that batting cage.

The new plant opened with four nightly tours. Visitors poured into the huge garage and loading area. Bringing the huge crowd up the stairs to the front door would never have worked. In the loading area, route trucks backed up to conveyors that lined the long wall. This would be a backward visit through the bakery. Visitors passed slicers and wrapping machines, then streamed upstairs toward that magnetic aroma of fresh bread baking. Huge final mixers ejected two thousand pounds of dough. The dough was cut loaf size, rose to fill pans in the 330 foot long proofing tunnel, then rode the conveyors into the twin 90 foot long ovens.

When baked loaves tumbled from the ovens bakers were waiting. They sliced still hot loaves lengthwise, removed the hot center, then generously daubed the two long pieces with butter. Another quick slice with the knife and each visitor received a slab. Eating hot buttered bread, fresh from the oven, was an experience to be long remembered.

Then visitors went back downstairs where another memorable experience awaited at a far end of the loading area. Mrs. Baird, now in her eighties, sat on a slightly raised platform and welcomed visitors. It was a rare experience for them, but an even more rewarding one for her. These were her customers, they loved her bread, and eagerly gathered close to tell her. They also wanted to see and talk with the amazing lady who started this business in her home kitchen.

Night Letter 'Magic'

With a huge new plant up and running it was time to add new territory. East Texas was the place to go.

Like a military campaign, the proposed new market must first be scouted. Sales supervisors and sales managers were brought in from other plants to help "case" the stores. How many bakeries were already in the market? How well were they serving their customers? How much space could be obtained on store shelves? Like military planners, the bakery scouts believed they could bring in fresher products and better service. That, and lots of advertising, is what they would promise the grocer on opening morning. "When bread is fresh, people eat more. That is going to mean more sales for you." Meanwhile, like an army about to invade and set people free, these scouts went to work. If grocers refused to give space on the bread rack, advertising would be no help.

Already in the 50s Paris, Texas, was a growing town. It

would be the first opened, then small towns to the East. The tactic was to tell no grocers in advance. Get the market scouted, schedule ads, and radio spots, then surprise the grocers. Trucks roll into town bright and early, show the grocers newspaper ads, and ask for space on the bread rack.

One of the ad agency "bright boys" suggested an innovation. "There's something new out from Western Union. They call it 'night letters.' Doesn't cost as much as telegrams. Delivered at night and in no rush. Let's send all the Paris grocers a night letter. Tell 'em we'll be at your store bright and early tomorrow morning, ready to serve you and your customers with Mrs Baird's Bread."

All heads nodded. Great idea. And out went the "night letters" the night before salesmen hit the stores.

"What the hell?" a grocer demanded the next morning. "We were almost asleep and the door bell rings. Western Union. Scared my wife something awful. Her mother is sick up in Oklahoma. And here comes your telegram."

A lot of apologizing went on that memorable morning. And not all grocers said, "Bring that bread on in." That would take time.

After the opening, the team moved out to call on grocers still balking. A lanky slow talking sales supervisor tackled a small grocery. The owner was a tiny black lady, gray haired and grandmotherly. "Now Auntie," the supervisor began, "you don't have Mrs Baird's Bread yet and your customers are going to want it."

"Am I related to you?" the lady asked.

Into his spiel, the supervisor didn't hear. "And Auntie, you will get fresh bread everyday. Not what they have been giving you before. And Auntie—"

This time she got through. "Am I related to you?"

He paused. "Well, no but—"

"Then, Mister, don't call me Auntie!"

Morris W., whose curly gray hair topped a friendly face, was one of the scouts. Before the opening he visited stores, meandered through the aisles, and got a good look at the bread rack. Since owners were always wary of strangers, Morris always bought pipe cleaners. They looked good on the expense account and besides, Morris smoked a pipe.

One grocer was out of pipe cleaners. "I got some coming," he promised. Morris thanked him and eased by to size up the bread rack on his way out.

On opening morning a salesman breezed in to get an okay. "Sure," the grocer said. "I been expecting you guys. Just put 'em over there on the rack. And tell that little curly headed guy we got in them pipe cleaners."

The Mystery Caller

Opening new markets was always a challenge. Usually a grocer's bread rack was full and it was not easy to get him to cut somebody's space and put your bread in. No one paid for space. To get that space on the shelf you had to convince the grocer his customers wanted a chance to buy your bread.

One of these was Port Arthur. Even though advertising was ample, some grocers still said "No" when it came to giving a newcomer space on already crammed shelves. This called for a novel approach, one that came out of a brainstorming session. It was aptly named "The Mystery Caller."

"The Mystery Caller is coming," radio spots announced. "If he comes to your house, and you have a loaf of Mrs Baird's Bread, the Mystery Caller will give you five dollars." This wouldn't work today when many people won't answer a knock on the door. But it worked then. Calls were made at random, in all neighborhoods rich or poor.

The message had not always gotten through. "You the who? Mystery Caller? What the devil is a mystery caller?" If the lady had the loaf of bread, she got five dollars. If she didn't, we left a coupon good for a loaf of bread. There was also a fervent plea: "You all come back now, you hear, we're gonna have that loaf of bread."

At a more fortunate home, "It's the Mystery Caller" created near panic.

"Hey," the man of the house yelled, "it's that Mystery Caller. He's out on the front porch. Get that loaf of Mrs Baird's Bread! Don't you leave now. She's gonna get it!"

The lady of the house arrived in a rush with the bread. "Well now thank you!" she beamed, as she accepted five dollars. "You want this loaf of bread?"

"No ma'am, you keep it. And thank you for buying Mrs Baird's Bread!"

It worked nicely. If no five dollar bills were passed out in a neighborhood, we tried again in a day or two. Gradually the word spread and so did the five dollar bills.

It was rewarding to work the poorer neighborhoods. Here you really hoped a knock on the door would find the right brand of bread. Here a five dollar bill was especially appreciated.

In a mostly black area, a knock on one door brought a weak, "Who is it?"

"I am the Mystery Caller."

"You the who?"

"The Mystery Caller."

"Well, I can't come to the door. It ain't locked. You all come on in."

The small hovel had a dirt floor. A man stretched on a cot asked, "Who you say you are?"

"I'm the Mystery Caller. If you have a loaf of Mrs Baird's Bread I'll give you five dollars."

THE GUNS NOBODY HEARD
23 YEARS THAT CHANGED AMERICA FOREVER

A long pause. "Man, I don't know what I got. Look over there in the cabinet. Might be some kind of bread in there."

There was not much in the cabinet. A can of beans with a spoon stuck in it. A box of oatmeal. No bread. Then, looking at the haggard man on the cot, maybe there was.

"Well, you are really lucky! Here's five dollars. And coupons good for two more loaves.

You keep on buying Mrs Baird's Bread!"

A faint smile. "Yes, Sir! I sure will!"

Some days being the Mystery Caller could be disappointing. This was not one of them.

Trees

Meanwhile back at the Dallas plant problems popped up to spoil the serene aroma of baking bread. This time it was birds.

Four lovely hackberry trees lined a section of the parking area and these drew a daily assembly of birds. They were there at dawn, welcoming us with lilting tunes. When taking song breaks, they splattered parked cars or flocked over to the thrift store unloading area to dine on crumbs before the sweeper uppers arrived. Birds in that area were not good for sanitation.

A "bird man" had the solution. "We'll put out some harmless stuff over by the trees where they flock," he advised. "Won't hurt 'em, just make 'em woozy. They'll stagger around like drunks. Birds are pretty sharp. They'll see those woozy birds staggerin' around and they'll get the Hell out."

So the bird cocktails were put out under the bright green hackberry trees. Immediately the daily assemblage began to shrink. Almost like some other bakery was serving better cocktails. Then the telephone rang. An environmental group had called the city. Birds were being mistreated. Several members had seen birds staggering beneath the trees at the parking area. Make them stop doing whatever they are doing to those poor birds.

So the "bird man" was ordered to cut off the cocktails. "But we're so close," he protested. "Most of the birds are gone and those few remaining are not hurt in any way. As soon as they're all cleared out we'll stop the juice and you'll still have your pretty shade trees and no birds.'

But with the environmentalists persistent, the orders were firm. Enough already with the bird juice. And back came the birds, with perhaps extra fly ins who had heard about the cool shade trees and the nearby area where bread crumbs were there for the picking. Just socialize in the cool trees, watch the unloading area, then get over there and pig out.

With the bird man gone and the birds flocking back, something had to be done. A chain saw was the answer. Down went the hackberries. Now there were no birds and no cool and verdant hackberries. The environmentalists won, and then again, maybe they lost.

Times a'Changin'

As war time faded, life across America was changing rapidly. A sizzler steak and baked potato lunch was still $1.75 but the owner had his marking pencil ready.

Advertising was changing too. Especially outdoor as narrow roads gave way to divided highways and speeding cars. One sign company battled the trend. It created a triangular metal sign that turned slowly in the breeze. This prompted an angry call and a quick trip to east Texas.

Strange problem here. The roadside spinning sign was two hundred yards from the lady's front porch. To see it she had to walk out on the front porch, move to the steps, and look left. When we knocked, she came out a hurry. "I want you to take that sign down!" she ordered, angrily. "That spinning thing is driving me crazy."

It came down. And so did the others. Cars were moving fast now, over on the wider new highways. Speed limits moved up.

Now drivers had no time to look at little signs.

Back at the bakery, the general manager decided a conference room was urgently needed. "We've got no place for department head meetings," he reasoned. The result was a large conference room with a long polished table fringed by comfortable padded chairs.

When office folks and department heads had gone for the day Shorty, the custodian moved in to check and clean this fancy room. He parked his sweeper, sat down at head of the long table, and slapped his hand down on the polished surface. "Something ain't right here, folks," he announced like a pompous CEO. "Something been goin' on with the money. I ain't gettin' any of it!"

One time consuming part of the advertising job was handling calls from people who wanted to sell ideas. An eager man called to say he had an idea that would triple bread sales in grocery stores. "I can't tell you over the phone. I'll come in there but I gotta be sure you won't steal my idea."

Usually it was best to politely refuse. The "idea" might be something already in the works.

Perhaps a tag line on an upcoming TV commercial. But the man was so fervent we relented.

"You got fresh bread aroma all over this bakery," the man announced, his eyes glowing. "You even blow it out there on Mockingbird Lane and Central Expressway. Well, what you got to do—and this is my idea— you put that fresh bread aroma in the grocery store. Right on the bread rack."

Great idea, mister. And *how* do you do that?

The man shrugged. "You figure that out! I'm givin' you the idea."

"Okay, then here's another idea. Let's sell rides to the moon. Now that's my idea and you figure out how to get 'em there."

THE GUNS NOBODY HEARD
23 YEARS THAT CHANGED AMERICA FOREVER

The man wasn't too happy when he left. Maybe that wasn't the way to treat a customer but going to the moon seemed just as ridiculous. Only it wasn't. Astronaut Armstrong may have taken along a loaf of fresh bread.

Other ridiculous ideas emerged about bread. When bakery executives met at conferences, they could talk about industry problems but never pricing. Their goal was to increase bread consumption. And they worked at it hard. At lunch, plates of hot rolls were eagerly eaten. But as lunch ended rolls still remained. A grinning baker carefully broke every roll in half. "Bust 'em," he advised. "That keeps 'em from serving them again. And makes 'em buy more rolls."

When pricing was mentioned, a pompous baker said, "Well, I think the economy is settled down. Prices aren't going to change."

"Don't be so sure," the head of one of the nation's top baking companies said. "One of these days bread will be a dollar a loaf."

The bakers laughed. That was ridiculous. Just like going to the moon.

Into the 'Idea' Den

Right off the boss said, "Don't be spending time trying to come up with advertising ideas. That's why we have the agency."

So it was time to meet this advertising agency.

They were down on Cedar Springs on the top floor of a two story building. In their future was a fabulous suite of offices in a downtown tower. But right now they were up close and personal on Cedar Springs. And on this first visit they were gathered at windows, nervously looking west.

A tornado blasted down Hines Boulevard, seemed to hesitate and head our way, then veered back North. It was a preview that years ahead with these folks would be turbulent but that we would do some movin' and shakin'.

The agency head was Morris Hite, who didn't look like the creative type but was one of the best. "When I was a boy up in Oklahoma," Morris related, "a man with a lot of money rounded up some of us. He said we were brighter than most." The man's aim was to give these bright kids the educational

THE GUNS NOBODY HEARD
23 YEARS THAT CHANGED AMERICA FOREVER

material he felt they needed. "He had files of Printer's Ink magazines," Morris recalled. "Each issue had a feature 'I learned About Advertising From That'. I read 'em all." Obviously Morris learned. While his proteges labored, the sponsor worked at his typewriter.

"He had the penthouse suite," Morris said. "Lots of bright sun. And he sat there nude and banged away at his typewriter." Morris learned, served in World War II, and now headed Tracy Locke Advertising. Now it was our agency, with cubby hole offices and pluggers in each one striving to come up with ideas. Hopefully to sell bread.

"Iggy's in that one," our guide said. "He does all the art for Mrs Baird's bread. He wears a cowboy hat pushed back on his head, and he's quite a golfer." Open the door and there was Iggy, only he was wearing a beret. "Just a change of pace," he grinned. Iggy also created beautiful paintings sold in Santa Fe galleries. That came out when the *Dallas Morning News* ran a Sunday morning feature. Iggy golfed that morning. His caddy had seen the story in the *News* and was impressed.

"Gosh, Mr. Sahula Dyke," the caddy beamed. "I read that story about your paintings. I bet they are gonna be worth a lot of money when you die!"

"They will be," Iggy agreed, "and I can't wait."

There were copy writers hidden away with food probably slipped under doors. They were back there somewhere, knocking out adjectives, verbs and other stuff they work with. Later we would find they were a talented bunch.

Account executives were the buffers between the agency and us clients. Like a lion tamer with whip and chair, they kept us at bay until the folks behind them solved the problems. Sometimes they failed, chairs were knocked aside, and the account was gone. Mrs Baird's would not be one but we kicked the chair a few times.

Our first account exec was Bill James. No relation. Bill was stocky and afraid of nobody. An infantry major, he and a sergeant recaptured a half track under enemy fire. "It was out there," Bill said, "and damned if we were going to let the Germans keep it."

THE GUNS NOBODY HEARD
23 YEARS THAT CHANGED AMERICA FOREVER

Bill had some interesting theories about advertising and merchandising. They are still good today. "Advertising," he said, "brings customers to the product. Merchandising takes the product to customers." He frowned at ads that extolled a company; ads that bragged about a company rather than the products it sold. This is called 'institutional advertising.' "It is like peeing down your leg. It gives you a nice warm feeling but nobody notices it."

To get his job with Tracy Locke, Bill first worked a year on a Borden milk route. Our first flight together was on a Douglas DC-3, the same bird I had flown in Kansas. This time we were seated back in the tail dragger, looking up the slanted walkway as the tall, eager stewardess took names. They did that in those days. Why we never knew.

Clipboard poised she asked Bill, "Sir, what is your last name?"

"James"

Then I spoke up. "Hey, that is *my* last name!"

The stewardess brightened. "And Sir, your first name?"

"William."

Again I interrupted. "Hey, William is my middle name!"

And Bill exclaimed. "And what is your first name?"

"Joseph."

"Well how about that!" Bill said. "Joseph is my middle name!"

All this was true, and we knew it, but the stewardess was excited. Swaying in the aisle as the tail dragger taxied she announced, "Ladies and gentlemen, you are not going to believe this!" Then she went through the routine. It sounded like "Who's on first" but the passengers laughed. In the back end of a DC-3, any excuse for a laugh helped.

'Birthin' Ideas

In *Gone with the Wind* Butterfly McQueen yelled, "Golly Miss Scarlet, I don't know nothin' about birthin' babies."

Down at Tracy Locke, they knew a lot about birthin' ideas but it took a lot of labor, especially on our account. Bakers were hung up on "freshness." Claims were pretty much the same. Television was black and white. So the "freshness" of flowers or piping hot bread grayed on TV screens.

Larry Dupont, creative director, listened intently to a challenge. "Can you make a sixty second commercial that tells the Mrs Baird's story?"

Sixty second commercials were okay, but most were eight second shorties. One Larry created featured a veteran Hollywood actor Addison Richards. Known for his honest, upright roles, Richards had conviction when he intoned, "We think it is important for you to know Mrs Baird's Bread stays fresh longer." Looking back, maybe it wasn't so important that a busy housewife chasing scampering kids needed to know Mrs Baird's Bread stayed fresh longer. Addison's severe tones made it sound that way.

But we needed more than that. Could Larry pack the "Mrs Baird's Story" in sixty seconds?

Larry could. Even worked in a horse and wagon. A modern little girl asking her mother, "Was there really Mrs. Baird?" And mama replied, "Oh yes, would you like to hear her story?" Of course the kid agreed, otherwise there would have been no commercial.

The commercial popped on with Mrs. Ninnie L. Baird at her kitchen stove. Now the boys first delivering bread in baskets. Next with a horse and wagon. Then her grown sons today checking quality. Finally, the four plants, all baking bread just like Mrs. Baird, now chairman of the board, wants it baked.

The commercial ran on TV and that was fine. But back there in one of those cubby holes researcher Jack Taylor and account man Richard Brown birthed an idea. "Let's take that commercial to Minneapolis. One of our competitors is not there so we start even. Get a room full of women and run our 'family story' commercial and our competitor's 'fresh bread' commercial. Offer the ladies a free loaf of bread, the one they choose, delivered to their home. Then, in another room, let's screen our 'fresh bread' commercial and the competitor's 'fresh bread' commercial. We'll make the same offer to the ladies."

Seventy five per cent of the women who had seen the 'story' commercial asked for a loaf of Mrs Baird's Bread. But the group that saw the two "fresh bread" commercials were not overly impressed. Only half chose our loaf. The idea was "birthed," but it was no time to pass out cigars. Bakers believed the best loaf they could bake, fresh on the grocer's shelf, was the story TV should tell. But credit W. Hoyt Baird with nodding his head and saying, "Okay, give it your best."

The story commercial ran on TV, interspersed with the usual "freshness" spots. Larry and his staff searched for a way to expand the family story. Hoyt Baird passed along family supervision of advertising to son Vernon Baird. Vernon was very convincing. Listen to him talk about Mrs Baird's Bread and you felt it was the best on the market. Next from one of those back offices where ideas were "birthed," out came a writer named Polly Bohmfalk. She wanted to hear first hand what Vernon Baird had to say about Mrs Baird's Bread. That might help her write convincing radio spots. Vernon talked and Polly listened. Then she wrote radio spots and suggested, "Let's get Vernon to do them."

Vernon had never faced a studio microphone before. But he was willing to try. He sat alone in the recording studio while Polly and our account exec watched through the window. Recording went so-so. Not too convincing. Then a suggestion. "Polly, go in there and sit across the table from Vernon. Let him read the commercial to you. Let him sell you face to face."

Voila! Now Vernon was *selling* a customer. The lines came alive.

Radio spots went well. So let's try television. Production went well, the commercials were convincing. They stressed that a family was closely involved in baking Mrs Baird's Bread. Their name was on the package. Each loaf was "baked with family pride." Before long Vernon was almost as well known across the state as the bread he sold. Maybe better. At a small filling station near Bryan, the gas pumper glanced at a credit card and said, "Mrs Baird's! Hey, Vernon was in here just the other day!"

Although Vernon moved up to president, he still did the TV and radio commercials. He became quite deft at it. Some of his fellow performers were not. In a diner sequence, an actress waitress moved on camera with toast. Her line was "Here's your toast, Vernon." It took twenty four takes for her to get it right.

And that is how an idea "birthed" in an advertising agency cubby hole, hopped out of its bassinet and "walked" across Texas.

Small World

Coupons have long been widely used in retailing. We printed large batches and bakeries used them in mailings to newcomers or thanking folks who wrote nice letters. We even sent a coupon if the letter was not nice. Once, when a man let me into a lane of stopped traffic, I hopped out of my car, walked back and handed him a coupon good for a loaf of Mrs Baird's Bread.

On a vacation we rode the train from Nuevo Laredo to Mexico City. It is a fun trip if you aren't in a hurry and speak a little Spanish. Rolling through the cactus flats the train pulled to a halt. We waited to learn the reason and asking yielded nothing. Then we saw the answer. The engineer and fireman were coming back through the tuna cactus. Each carried a shot gun and a rabbit. Later when we were ready to head for home, the train sat in the station for a frustrating long time. Finally the conductor came walking alongside the train, carefully inspecting the under areas. "What's going on," one frustrated passenger yelled. "We've been sitting here an hour!"

The conductor smiled up at him and replied, "*Hay mas tiempo que vida!*" Translated: "There is more time than we have life to live it."

But back to the coupons.

While in Mexico City, I noticed a "Pan Bimbo" bread truck approaching. I waved the driver over and handed him a coupon good for a loaf of Mrs Baird's Bread. He seemed puzzled and drove off inspecting the coupon. Neither of us dreamed that was an omen of things to come.

Years later, in 1998, Bimbo bought Mrs. Baird's Bakeries. Grupo Bimbo which now has 17 bakeries in the United States including Mrs Baird's in Texas and bakeries in California and Ohio. In addition to Mexican bakeries Grupo Bimbo is in 11 Latin American countries.

The vacant Dallas plant was recently shut down and operations moved to Fort Worth where Mrs. Baird baked her first loaves long ago. The vacant property was sold by Grupo to Southern Methodist University. One old timer, told of the sale, said, "I'm glad to see SMU buy that bakery. Some of them professors have half baked ideas."

Fire to Cool By

Until the mid 1950's most home dwellers sweltered in summer heat. Some tried "mildew machines," stuck in windows, that spewed water over a screen while air blew through. Attic fans vibrated and whirred, sucking in warm outside air and not really effective until the sun went down.

West of Dallas, in the then small town of Irving, a developer introduced a new idea. Rows of fairly well designed small houses, with three equally small bedrooms and strange structures in back yards. Slightly larger than an out house, each small tower had four slatted sides. Water flowed down these slats cooling heat sucked from the house. An electric motor in the tower supplied power. (If that is an incorrect interpretation you engineers buzz off.)

Not that we didn't have engineers. One was quietly helping draw plans for the electricity powered cars that now speed around tracks at Dallas-Fort Worth Airport. The cars are computer controlled. No drivers. As the automated cars make their rounds, smart alecks like to call, "Let me off at the next stop!"

But back to those dinky cooling towers. They were odd looking, but in July and August heat residents of "cooling tower hill" basked in cool air and wondered how the other half survived. It was with this kind of superior feeling we invited friends out from Dallas as our first dinner guests. Our trim little home had another neat feature: A sliding glass door with a superb view of the still bare dirt unfenced yard. And there in all its pristine glory was the gurgling cooling tower.

Dinner went beautifully. First toddies while we basked in cool air and all outside sizzled in evening heat. Then dinner was served. Wine flowed. As glasses were lifted in toasts, a neighbor ran into the back yard. He waved frantically and pointed. Little tongues of flame leaped and danced across the yard in a conga line.

"Quick! Call the fire department!" our hostess yelled. "The yard's on fire! Our house is next."

One of our guests shrugged. "Nah! Don't call 'em. That is just gas escaping. Must be a crack in the line. A spark from that cooling tower touched it off. It's not going anywhere."

"Are you sure?"

"Sure, it won't hurt anything. By now somebody in that crowd has called the gas company. They'll come and turn off the gas."

So we resumed toasting while neighbors and people from the next county surged around our yard and watched the dancing flames. Some, not too polite, stared at us diners looking cool behind closed doors and windows.

The secret was right there among them, our cooling tower gurgling contentedly while flames danced.

Death Across the River

As we moved into the 1960s, son Mark was old enough to put away the air rifle and tackle a shot gun. A second hand twelve gauge automatic seemed perfect so we bought one at Cullem and Boren in downtown Dallas.

A friend in Georgetown invited us down for quail hunting. That was great sport. Judy, his brown spotted bird dog, was one of the smartest. As we walked three in line Judy zig zagged out front, head high for scent of birds. When Doc whistled, she whirled and came racing back. She responded beautifully and that may have been prompted by the collar she wore. It was an "electric" collar. If Doc touched a button, Judy got a light shock. If she kept going, she got another. Now Doc seldom touched the button. Judy raced eagerly far ahead, then dropped to a stiff point as she cornered quail. She held the point steadily until Doc arrived and nudged the quail. They came up fast, guns roared, and Judy was off to bring the birds to her proud owner.

THE GUNS NOBODY HEARD
23 YEARS THAT CHANGED AMERICA FOREVER

This was great fun. When we could, and quail were in season, we headed eagerly South to join Doc and Judy on another hunt. Judy continued to star until one day late in the season. This time she wandered too far ahead. She ignored Doc's whistle. The electric collar was of no avail. Perhaps Judy was too far away. Then she wheeled and headed back. Head held high, she trotted toward us ready for our praise. But not this time. What she carried was not a quail. It was a white leghorn hen. Judy may have been in a hen house. Now she was in the dog house.

We headed back to Dallas hoping Judy reformed in a hurry. Meanwhile where we could go to shoot? Even the best shooters, without practice, lose their skill.

Then an idea sparked. The Trinity river meandered through the mud flats between Irving and Dallas. Usually a shallow trickle, it was flanked on each side by dank rolling and untenable terrain. Later flood control would bring in commercial developers. But for now this was a perfect place to fire our guns.

On late afternoons Mark and I brought our guns and walked down into the wasteland. In the distance the Dallas skyline stretched with its flying Red Horse. Here in the river bottoms, clouds of blackbirds swirled by, back from feeding on some farmer's crop and heading for roosting spots. We fired as they swept past, hitting some and missing many. The birds we downed left no gap in the dark clouds. We were honing our skills, getting ready for quail when Judy got out of rehab.

On the Dallas side another shooter was about to enter our practice range. He ordered an Italian 6.5 Mannlicher-Carcano Model 1891 rifle by mail from Chicago, bought ammunition, and came to the Dallas side to "sight in" his rifle. We might have been on opposite sides of the river at the same time. The "boom" of an occasional rifle across the river created no problem. Not as long as no bullets came our way. While we shot at blackbirds, this rifle shooter on the Dallas side probably aimed at paper plates or a box stuck in the mud.

His future target was far more frightening. His name was Lee Harvey Oswald.

Lunch with a Lion

Most club luncheons are routine affairs. The speaker sits a head table with the club president and program chair Members cluster around tables and, as chicken and pea served, wonder if this is going to be one of those rare outstanding programs.

When the lion arrived members of the Dallas Adverl League knew this program would be different.

The lion came in on a leash, casually guided by a man who obviously was not the speaker. At his command the lion, a fully grown female, stretched out on the carpet next to the dance floor and began to snooze.

My guest was Bob Stanford, talented ad director for Seven Eleven. Bob had a great sense of humor but was not ready for what was about to happen. We sat in a booth about fifteen feet from the lioness. We hoped she had been fed.

The speaker, sorting notes at the head table, glanced

uneasily at the snoozing lion. It was no part of her show. The lion man was probably sneaking in a plug for an upcoming movie about a friendly lion. Or maybe he was planning a flick about a lion that attended civic club meetings.

The scene was the Century Room in Dallas' downtown Adolphus Hotel. The Century Room was famous for Dot Franey and her ice skaters. At nightly floor show time the polished dance floor slid silently out of the way to reveal an ice rink. Lights lowered and out swirled Dot and her dancers on flashing blades.

Today, at the Ad League luncheon, the dance floor was in place with tables to handle the over size group of ad folks. The speaker was a famous copy writer from a Chicago agency. She was here to tell us about the surge of inspiration that had helped move her client's products off the shelves. Her talk was lively and, at the proper moment, she motioned for the lights to dim. Her slide show was about to begin. A club member hurried to the small control room to lower the lights. In the darkened room, he accidentally flipped the Dot Franey floor show switch.

The highly polished dance floor began to move, slowly exposing ice. Funny at first, then all realized the retracting floor would dump tables on the ice and then down would go the head table. The floor moved slowly, passing the now awakened lion who sat on haunches to watch as tables toppled and dishes smashed on ice.

Now the moving floor reached the head table. As the floor slid under front legs, the table tilted. Dishes and flower arrangements slid forward, then smashed on the ice. The speaker scrambled from her chair and hopped on the ledge behind it. Her companions were already there.

Only the lion was calm.

Two Guns on Elm Street

Another lion, this time unseen, was moving across Texas. It was the lion of political hatred. Some Texans had already forgotten how courageously President Jack Kennedy had stopped the Cuban crisis. Some openly hated the President. Not many, it is true, but enough to spread concern about the President's scheduled visit to Dallas and Fort Worth. Native son Vice President Lyndon Johnson was in for some hissing and reported spitting when he visited Dallas. Obviously the natives, at least some of them, were restless.

Strange things happened, forewarnings of worse to come. Retired General Edwin A. Walker, who had put down civil unrest in Mississippi, moved into a house on Cedar Springs. It was a quiet neighborhood, especially at nighttime, until a sniper took a shot at the General as he wrote at his desk. The sniper missed. That was a bad omen.

Some urged President Kennedy to cancel his proposed trip

to Dallas and Fort Worth. There was too much hate, they warned. But a vast majority urged him to "come on down" and promised he would get a warm welcome.

There was one protester who did not agree. He bought a full page ad in the *Dallas Morning News* to protest the President's scheduled visit. It was not a "warm welcome" but rather just the opposite. It urged the President to stay out of Dallas.

But as you know President Kennedy came anyway. He was warmly welcomed at Love Field, then went over to Fort Worth where the welcome was equally "Texas-sized."

If one had a lot of work to do and was glad Texans were behaving like ladies and gentlemen, the President's coming and going were of no great concern. In fact it slipped my mind. And that could have earned me a set of hand cuffs and who knows how many nights in jail. It may still not be too late for the FBI to come calling.

But after over 40 years I'll tell you what I've told no one before.

Quail season had started. We tested the "experienced" 12 gauge automatic down in the river flats. Now and then it failed to eject shell casings. That would spoil a quail hunt so it was time to take the gun to downtown Cullum & Boren for repair.

I put the gun in its case, making sure it had no shells, and stowed it in the car trunk. The next day turned up with an easy schedule so, shortly before noon, I drove downtown and parked the car. Removing the gun case I headed for Cullum & Boren. It was just a few blocks away. I'd leave the gun, drive back to the bakery, and still have time for lunch.

Both sides of Elm Street were lined with people. All expectantly looked east.

An amiable fellow smiled as I arrived swinging the gun case. "What's going on?" I asked.

THE GUNS NOBODY HEARD
23 YEARS THAT CHANGED AMERICA FOREVER

"The President's coming," he said. "Should be through here in about fifteen minutes."

Fifteen minutes? That was no good. He might come any minute so I shouldn't try to cross Elm until the cars had passed. I decided to come back another day. Maybe tomorrow.

The drive back to the bakery did not take long. I parked on our lot and walked across Mockingbird to the Cafeteria.

"Isn't it terrible," the cashier called.

"What's terrible?"

"Haven't you heard? Someone just shot the President."

I ate in numbed silence. Suppose I had waited for the President to pass? After Oswald's shot, anyone downtown with a gun case would have been in big trouble. No questions, just slammed down and handcuffed.

There was one positive thought. While some disagreed with the President's policies, no one dreamed somebody would try to kill him. If there had been any such thought anyone who saw me standing there with a gun case would have yelled "Police!"

I'm glad they didn't.

Tears in the Afternoon

When President Lincoln was assassinated his return to Illinois was a long, slow train ride with crowds at small towns waiting to pay their respects. But this was different. In near panic there was a rush to swear in Vice President Lyndon Johnson and get the 707 in the air. Those who killed Kennedy might strike again. Unlike the train that chugged slowly back to Illinois the jet streaked toward Washington at 600 miles an hour.

Few realized the Dallas tragedy marked the end of an era. Texas and the nation plunged into anger and apprehension. War was again possible. Had Russia conspired to send Lee Harvey Oswald back to Texas to kill the President? Were others here, waiting to strike? Were atomic missiles being readied? There was a new feeling across the land, one destined to haunt us through the years and even as you read this.

We Texans endured the storm of hate that rolled toward us. Time would reveal we were like the rest of the nation—

different ideas at the voting booth but respect for our President. A twisted soul with a mail order rifle had chosen Dallas as the place to do his killing.

We had enjoyed a unique "island of time" between World War II and the crack of Oswald's rifle. Today Dallas, where it all began, is apprehensive beneath its hustle and bustle. So is the rest of Texas and America.

Was Professor Crawford correct, back in 1939, when he predicted one hundred years of war? We hope not but, if you listen quietly you might hear the guns.

also available from publishamerica
IGNITED VERSES
by Felicia Rogers

Life is poetry. Poetry is life. *Ignited Verses* is a collection of poems that contains a piece of the author's heart and soul. It is intended to ignite your passion to life and love.

"Poeta nascitur, non fit…A poet is born, not made."

Felicia has been a poet most of her life but has taken her God-given talent more seriously the past several years.

Her poem "Sydne" appeared in poetry anthologies, *TIMELESS VOICES* and *INTERNATIONAL WHO'S WHO IN POETRY*, published in Maryland, USA, last 2006. She received an Editor's Choice Award for this poem. It is also one of the poems included in a *CD-SONGS OF POETRY* released this year by http://www.poetry.com

Paperback, 63 pages
6" x 9"
ISBN 1-4241-7974-2

About the author:

The daughter of a doctor and an insurance underwriter, she works as a nurse in a local community hospital and a nursing home.

Felicia wants to be remembered as a child of God who has learned, loved and left a legacy through her poems.

available to all bookstores nationwide.
www.publishamerica.com

also available from publishamerica
SECRET SACRIFICES
by Cynthia Hall

Maggie Brown's ten-year-old secret is in danger of being revealed when her daughter Tracey is abducted. Desperate to find her, Maggie contacts Tracey's biological father, Matt Sanford. The unsuspecting father uses his law enforcement skills as he would with any routine kidnaping case to help locate Tracey. Maggie and Matt rush against time and a powerful tropical storm to get to Tracey before she is taken away forever. While Maggie and Matt's undercover journey leads them into dangerous twists and turns involving a devious Caribbean kidnaping ring and a bad cop, Tracey is fighting her own battle when she is brought into a questionable environment of abuse and uncertainty. Maggie's frantic search forces her to make decisions that could shake the stability of her private world. Tracey is faced with finding strength beyond her comprehension, and Matt must decide if he is able to forgive.

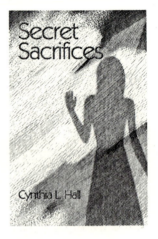

Paperback, 195pages
6" x 9"
ISBN 1-4241-7257-8

About the author:

When Cynthia L. Hall began work on her debut novel, *Secret Sacrifices*, she worked for a local sheriff's department, which gave her great insight into law enforcement and helped with the details. Cynthia's writing includes human interest stories and freelance photojournalism. She and her husband live in Ohio. They have one daughter.

available to all bookstores nationwide.
www.publishamerica.com

also available from publishamerica
LORD OF ALL SCIENCE
ESSAYS FOR GOOD
by Ralph Fudge

Lord of All Science is a collection of fourteen essays that have the purpose of doing good by first pointing out why the author believes in God as a result of studying science, and second, by offering knowledge and ideas collected over his lifetime. The first chapter asks the question, "Does God Exist?" and discusses solid reasons for believing that He does. The next three chapters point out how the great order found in nature and the extreme complexity of life both support the belief that God exists. The remaining ten chapters discuss ideas such as thinking, knowledge, wisdom, and education, as well as good and evil, human nature, the benefits of work, human weight control, and finally, happiness through the development of good relationships with family and friends. A lot of Christian doctrine is presented and discussed. The book was written at the suggestion of the author's friends.

Paperback, 177 pages
5.5" x 8.5"
ISBN 1-4241-5028-0

About the author:

Ralph Fudge was born in the small town of Blakely, Georgia. He has been married 38 years and has two children and a grandson. Ralph has been a teacher of high school and college science courses for 33 years and is active in his church in Thomasville, Georgia.

available to all bookstores nationwide.
www.publishamerica.com

also available from publishamerica
LIFE-CHANGING MESSAGES
WITH ETERNAL DIVIDENDS
by Tonya Fleming

Who is this God that many speak about, and where did he come from? God's Maker was a four-letter word. In other words God was formed by one word, and the word is love. His Maker from the beginning of time declared God's creation. This word has more power and life than any other word. This word formed an everlasting Spirit, the Spirit of God. The billion-dollar question has been answered. Where did God come from? When these four letters connected, it brought forth so much power that it created God. God's creator lives on the inside of him. God's in love! And he's in love with you.

Paperback, 48 pages
6" x 9"
ISBN 1-60474-559-2

About the author:

Tonya L. Fleming was born December 14, 1963, in Bellville, Texas. She is a graduate of Temple High School, better known as Tonya Shaw. Fleming is seeking an associate's degree in communications and a master's degree in English at the University of Phoenix. She is an author, a preacher of righteousness, a wife and a mother of two. Fleming is the founder of House of Compassion ministries. She is an intercessor. In other words, she stands in the gap between God and man praying for souls to be saved and people to be delivered from burdens and yokes that are destroying their lives. Look for *Messages from Your First Love* coming soon.

available to all bookstores nationwide.
www.publishamerica.com